baby and toddler
cookbook

baby and toddler
cookbook

RACHAEL ANNE HILL

photography by Tara Fisher

RYLAND
PETERS
& SMALL

LONDON NEW YORK

Dedication
To Barnaby and Brook

Senior Designer Sonya Nathoo
Editor Céline Hughes
Production Manager Patricia Harrington
Location Research Emily Westlake
Art Director Leslie Harrington
Publishing Director Alison Starling

Food Stylist Joss Herd
Prop Stylist Liz Belton
Indexer Sandra Shotter

Consultant Pediatric Nutritionist
 Bridget L. Wardley MS, RD
US Recipe Editor Susan Stuck

First published in the United States in 2008
by Ryland Peters & Small, Inc.
519 Broadway, 5th Floor
New York, NY 10012
www.rylandpeters.com

10 9 8 7 6 5 4 3 2 1

Text © Rachael Anne Hill 2008
Design and photographs
© Ryland Peters & Small 2008

Printed in China

ISBN: 978 1 84597 588 3

Notes
• Spoon measurements are level, unless otherwise
specified.
• Ovens should be preheated to the specified
temperature. Recipes in this book were tested using a
regular oven. If using a convection oven, follow the
manufacturer's instructions.

Author's acknowledgments
No book comes to fruition without a team of
truly hardworking and dedicated people and
this one is no exception. A huge thank you to
Liz Barr for being the fabulously competent,
hilariously funny, and ever positive person that
she is; to Céline Hughes for all her patience and
dedication to detail; and to Alison Starling
for making it possible in the first place.

Library of Congress Cataloging-in-Publication Data

Hill, Rachael Anne.
  Baby and toddler cookbook / Rachael Anne Hill ;
photography by Tara Fisher.
     p. cm.
  Includes index.
  ISBN 978-1-84597-588-3
  1. Cookery (Baby foods) 2. Baby foods. 3. Infants--
Nutrition. 4. Children--Nutrition. I. Title.
  TX740.H56 2008
  641.5'622--dc22

                              2007039655

**Neither the author nor the
publisher can be held responsible
for any claim arising out of the
use or misuse of the information
in this book. Always consult your
pediatrician if you have any
concerns about your child's
health or nutrition.**

contents

introduction

The foods a baby eats in his first few months can not only influence his taste buds and preferences for life, but also have a profound effect on his short- and long-term health. Little wonder then that many new parents can feel a little daunted at the prospect of weaning their child onto solid foods. There's a lot to think about: How do I know when my child is ready? Which foods are safe to give, and when? What texture should they be? How much should I give? When should I give it? Armed with a few key facts—all of which are clearly and concisely laid out in the first chapter of this book—there is no need for any parent to feel worried about weaning. It is a fantastic and unique opportunity to lay down some nutritional foundations that will benefit your little one for the rest of his life and introduce him to one of life's greatest pleasures—food!

homemade or commercially prepared?

There are usually two main reasons why a parent chooses commercially prepared or storebought baby food instead of homemade. The first is convenience. If you are away from home, on vacation, or if you find yourself stretched for time, it can be a godsend, but take a look at the expiration date and you'll see that the food is often designed to last for up to two years. Such a long shelf life is achieved by heating the food to high temperatures, then allowing it to cool. This sterilizes the contents but also destroys some of the nutrients in the process. Commercial varieties also tend to be very bland in taste. This is deliberately done to reduce the chances of your baby rejecting them, which would make you unlikely to buy them again. A baby weaned predominantly on bland, processed foods will develop a taste for them. Therefore, although the temptation to reach for the jarred stuff can be huge, I strongly urge you to resist.

Remember that the weaning process is not just about feeding your baby—it's also about educating her palate. So even if that spoonful of homemade purée comes back out of your baby's mouth as quickly as it went in, you can still view it as a success. She may not eat it the first time, but she has experienced the taste and texture of the food and the more she does this, the broader her palate will be, ensuring that she develops a healthy, adventurous love of food.

The second reason parents might opt for commercially prepared baby food is that they believe it contains all the essential nutrients and therefore the balanced diet their baby needs. This is not necessarily the case. The healthiest baby foods are the ones you make yourself, since you can be sure of using the best ingredients with no thickeners or additives. They'll taste far better and of course, they're cheaper too!

Introducing solids

There is no "right" age to introduce solids, since every baby differs. In general, introduction of solids is recommended between four and six months of age. The best advice is to follow your instincts, let your baby guide you (see below), and if in doubt, consult your pediatrician. In any case, starting weaning before four months have passed from your baby's due date is not recommended as the digestive and immune systems have not sufficiently developed. Starting too early can also increase the risk of allergies and obesity in later

life. Waiting too long to start weaning can result in some babies having difficulty eating foods with lumps later on and could also result in nutritional deficiencies, since after six months your baby needs more iron and nutrients than breast milk or formua alone can provide.

Signs that your baby is ready for solids
• Your baby starts demanding feeds more often.
• He still seems hungry after his usual milk feeding.
• He starts to wake in the night for an extra feeding when previously he slept through.
• He takes an interest in the foods you and the family are eating.
• He starts to chew hands excessively and put things in his mouth.

DID YOU KNOW?
The senses of taste and smell develop in a baby about 28 weeks into pregnancy. What a mother consumes during pregnancy can affect the odor of the amniotic fluid around the baby. So even before a baby is born it becomes familiar with many flavors.

hygiene and equipment

Hygiene

Cleanliness is always of paramount importance in a kitchen, but never more so than when you are cooking for a baby. This is because children are especially vulnerable to bacteria that can cause food poisoning. So always wash spoons, bowls, and any other equipment such as ice cube trays, food processors etc. thoroughly (use the steam cycle on your dishwasher if you have one) and either dry using a clean towel or let them air dry. It is particularly important to keep your baby's spoons, bottles, nipples, and sippy cups extremely clean as they can all be a breeding ground for bacteria.

Always store, prepare, and cook food safely and keep the kitchen and the equipment you use in the kitchen spotlessly clean. Wipe surfaces regularly using an antibacterial agent and clean the inside of your fridge regularly.

Preparation

• Always wash your hands before preparing food, after touching raw meat, fish, and raw eggs, and before feeding your child.

• Use separate chopping boards for meat and fish and another for fruit and vegetables.

• Wash all fruit and vegetables thoroughly before eating.

Equipment

You'll probably have most of the equipment you need already, but here are a few baby-friendly items that will come in handy:

• The baby essentials which you'll already have from the last few months—bottles, nipples, and a couple of beakers.

• A few strong, small plastic spoons.

• A few plastic bowls, preferably with suction cups on the bottom to prevent them becoming items of clothing! You may also want small plastic plates for toddlers.

• A few bibs and clean cloths. Pelican bibs—those that have a deep lip at the bottom—are particularly useful for catching dropped food.

• A mini-blender or food processor and/or a handheld blender for puréeing.

• A fine sieve with a metal mesh (first food purées may still need to be pressed through a sieve after being blended).

• A handheld ricer—this is a bit like a cross between a strainer and a grater. It has a wind-up handle that pushes the food through a selection of metal disks, each with a different sized hole. It is particularly useful if you are cooking in small quantities and ideal in the early stages of weaning as it holds back the husks or skins of foods which young babies are unable to digest.

• Bendy ice cube trays for storing baby portions, mini-containers with snap-on lids suitable for freezing (these are handy to use as feeding pots, too), and small freezer bags.

• A steamer—a multi-layered steamer that fits on top of a pan—or an electric steamer will enable you to cook a number of foods at once (which is ideal if you are also cooking for other members of the family). However, a simple collapsible stainless steel steamer placed over a pan of boiling water will do the job just as well with a lid placed on top.

• A V-shaped cushion to help prop up young babies.

• A highchair or a clip-on chair which can be clamped to the table. Clip-on chairs can be particularly useful to carry with you in the car in case friends, relatives, or restaurants don't have a highchair.

cooking, storing, and freezing

Steaming
Steaming is an excellent way to cook foods as it helps to preserve the taste and the nutrients in foods better than any other cooking method. When preparing fruit and vegetables, cooking them until they are soft will make them much easier to purée, but as your child gets older, cook them a little less to retain as many nutrients as possible.

Boiling
If you boil foods, use a very small amount of water and cook them for the minimum time allowed as overcooking can destroy valuable vitamins. Put some of the cooking liquid (and hence the nutrients) back in when you make purées.

Baking
Baking can be another excellent of way of ensuring that you retain as many nutrients as possible within the food. It's a particularly useful and labor-saving method for cooking sweet potatoes, potatoes, and squashes. Simply prick the skin with a fork, bake until tender, then scoop out and mash or purée the flesh.

Microwaving
Put chopped vegetables or fruit into a microwaveable dish, add a little water, cover, and cook on full power for just enough time to make them tender. Some research suggests that microwaving destroys many antioxidants within the food so where possible try to steam, bake, or boil instead.

Storing and freezing
Very small batches of baby food can be difficult to blend and process so make large amounts and freeze what you don't need in small containers or ice cube trays. This of course has the added advantage of ensuring that you can always have a

delicious, homemade meal ready in minutes. Simply cook and process the food (if necessary), cover, and let cool (never put warm food in the freezer), then freeze immediately. If freezing in an ice cube tray, wait until the food has frozen hard then pop the frozen purées out and put them in a freezer bag clearly labeled with what the food is and the date it was made. This will help to ensure that you don't give your baby food that has passed its shelf life (use baby foods within six weeks of freezing).

Note: At all times, keep raw meat, fish, and eggs away from other foods.

Thawing

Remove the number of frozen purée cubes you think you will need from the freezer bag, defrost in a microwave, or heat gently in a pan. Alternatively, remove them in advance and let them defrost naturally at room temperature for 2 hours or let defrost overnight in the fridge. Defrosted baby food stored in the fridge must be used within 24 hours.

Reheating

Spoon out the amount you think your baby will eat and heat this. Don't heat a large amount of thawed food because you will only have to throw it away—it's unsafe to reheat previously warmed food. Never refreeze any food that's been warmed or previously frozen.

Heat foods thoroughly until they are piping hot. Stir well (particularly if using a microwave as this method of heating can result in "hotspots" within the food). Let cool slightly and test that the food is lukewarm before offering it to your baby. A baby's mouth is very sensitive so anything warmer could feel too hot and put them off eating.

kitchen essentials

All the recipes in this book are made from common, everyday ingredients. However, stocking your cupboards with these essentials below should help to ensure that you always have what you need. Refer to the charts on pages 18–21 for which foods and drinks to introduce and when.

Bread and crackers
- Whole-grain and white bread, pita bread, English muffins.
- Breadsticks.
- Rye crackers, water biscuits, oatcakes.

Pasta and noodles
- Stock a number of different shapes of pasta such as penne, spaghetti, vermicelli, farfalle, fettuccine, fusilli, lasagne.
- Noodles of any sort.

Rice, grains, and cereals
- Rice cereal, white and brown rice, risotto rice.
- Pearl barley.
- Couscous and bulgur wheat.
- Rolled oats, oat flour, semolina, cornmeal.

Commercial breakfast cereals
- Choose cereals that have a low sugar content and that are made with rice, oats, and wheat.

Beans and lentils
- Any canned or dried beans including red kidney beans, cannellini beans, butter beans, navy beans, aduki beans, borlotti, pinto, chickpeas.
- Red and green lentils.
- Reduced-sodium and low-sugar canned baked beans.

Dairy
- Fresh whole milk, ideally organic.
- Cream.
- Full-fat plain yogurt, low-sugar fruit yogurts, Greek yogurt.
- Cottage cheese, ricotta cheese, mild cheddar.

Meat, poultry, fish, and eggs
- Ham.
- Good-quality ground beef and ground lamb.
- Turkey slices (fresh from the deli counter, not processed).
- Chicken—buying individually packaged chicken breasts, legs, or wings is convenient, but good-quality, organic, outdoor-reared chicken (which, in my opinion, is the only stuff we should be buying both on animal welfare grounds, and also to ensure the best health of our children) can be extremely expensive. However, if you buy a whole chicken and either roast it whole or split it into breasts, thighs, and wings (if you are unsure of how to do this ask your butcher to do it for you), then freeze them, it is far more economical. Buying chicken in this way also has the added advantage of allowing you to make delicious, fresh broth from the bones. Aim to buy organic meat whenever possible (see page 33).
- Mackerel and sardines (packed in oil and fresh).
- Salmon (ideally wild or organic salmon fillets).
- Fresh and canned tuna.
- Cod.
- Haddock.
- Flounder.
- Organic or free-range eggs (omega-3 enriched if possible).

Fruit

- Any! Particularly apples, pears, plums, cherries, peaches, strawberries, raspberries, blackberries, kiwi fruit, oranges, limes, lemons, grapefruit, red grapes, avocado. And don't forget canned fruit in fruit juice (rather than syrup) and frozen mixed berries.
- Dried fruits including organic dried apricots, dates, figs, raisins, golden raisins. N.B. Nonorganic dried fruits are often coated with sulfur dioxide to preserve them and stop discoloration, but it also destroys vitamin B_1 (thiamine) and can cause adverse reactions, including asthma attacks, in some susceptible children.

Vegetables

- Potatoes, sweet potatoes, and yams.
- As many different colored vegetables as possible.
- Frozen vegetables (these can be just as nutritious as fresh ones and meals can be made from them in no time).
- Canned tomatoes and corn.

Fats and oils

- Virgin olive oil, sunflower oil, and vegetable oil (for cooking and baking).
- Extra virgin cold-pressed olive oil—this is the best, healthiest olive oil you can buy, since the way in which the oil is extracted from the olives ensures very little of the vitamins, minerals, antioxidants, and fatty acids are lost. However, it is best used cold as heat from cooking will kill the flavor.
- Sunflower margarine and polyunsaturated spread.
- Unsalted butter.

Baking and cooking ingredients

- Whole-wheat, all-purpose, self-rising, and bread flours.
- Baking powder.
- Baking soda.

Nuts and seeds*

- Unsalted peanuts, flaked and ground almonds, walnuts, brazil nuts, pecans, cashew nuts, hazelnuts, mixed nuts.
- Sunflower seeds, pumpkin seeds, sesame seeds, poppy seeds, flaxseeds.

*Only offer nuts and seeds to your baby after 7 months if there is no family history of allergies (see pages 22–25). Do not offer whole nuts because of the risk of choking.

Pantry essentials

- Low-salt, concentrated chicken, beef, and vegetable stock cubes or bouillon.
- Fresh garlic.
- Reduced-sodium soy sauce.
- Low-sugar tomato ketchup.
- Worcestershire sauce.
- Tomato paste, garlic purée.
- Olives.
- Balsamic vinegar, red wine vinegar.
- Pesto.
- Natural lemon juice.
- Good-quality dark chocolate (at least 70% cocoa solids).
- Cranberry sauce, completely natural, smooth peanut butter (see page 25), 100% fruit jam, honey (see page 27).
- Cornstarch.
- Unsweetened fresh fruit juices, not from concentrate.

Herbs and spices

- Mixed spice, ground ginger, ground cinnamon, mild paprika, mild curry powder, ground cumin.
- Fresh vanilla beans.
- Fresh and ground nutmeg.
- Dried mixed herbs, bay leaves, oregano, thyme.
- Fresh basil, flatleaf parsley, oregano, sage, mint.

when to introduce foods

This chart is an approximate guide only. When you introduce foods will depend a great deal on your baby's likes, dislikes, possible allergies, intolerances, appetite etc. If in doubt, speak to your pediatrician.

FOOD	STAGE ONE: (APPROX. 4–6 MONTHS)	STAGE TWO: APPROX. 7–9 MONTHS	STAGE THREE: APPROX. 9–12 MONTHS	OVER 12 MONTHS
Texture The texture of your baby's food is extremely important. Always progress very gradually from one stage to the next.	Very smooth, slightly sloppy strained purées. As things progress, gradually offer slightly thicker, smooth but unstrained purées.	Gradually introduce different tastes, such as beans and puréed meat (important sources of iron). Different textures (minced and then chopped) can also be introduced as he begins to chew. As he gets older and begins to put foods in his own mouth, soft fingerfoods can be given, e.g. toast, cooked broccoli florets, carrot sticks, and pasta shapes, breadsticks, banana, pear.	Your baby should gradually become less dependent on milk and should have progressed to a more adult type of diet that is quite coarsely mashed, minced, and chopped. Introduce harder fingerfoods such as raw fruit and vegetables, but always be aware that small pieces can be a choking hazard.	Your child should now be progressing toward enjoying foods of normal textures. Keep introducing new tastes, textures, and temperatures through foods such as melon, dips, crunchy crackers, salad greens, ice cream, warm rice pudding.
Quantity The amount a baby eats varies a great deal from time to time and from child to child. These are suggestions but let your baby be your guide.	This stage is all about letting your baby get used to eating from a spoon and trying different tastes so don't worry about how much he eats. He will still be getting much of what he needs from his milk.	Three mini-meals per day of about 2–4 tablespoons per meal.	Three main meals (which contain a wide variety of different foods) of about 3–6 tablespoons per meal as well as one or two healthy snacks.	Three main meals (which contain a wide variety of different foods) as well as one or two healthy snacks.
Cereals, grains, and beans	Babies under six months should not eat wheat or other gluten-containing cereals, e.g. barley or rye, as early exposure to gluten may increase the risk of celiac disease. Start with nonwheat cereals and low-fiber grains, e.g. rice cereal, homemade rice purées. Try small amounts of well-cooked red lentils.	Wheat-based products, e.g. bread, pasta, crispbreads* (see page 25). Lentils and small amounts of less fibrous beans such as lima beans. Avoid using too many unrefined grains as the fiber content is high making them very bulky and filling, which could result in a lack of calories and nutrients in the diet.	Introduce chickpeas, split peas, kidney and navy beans. Red and green lentils. Avoid using too many unrefined grains as the fiber content is high making them very bulky and filling, which could result in a lack of calories and nutrients in the diet.	Once your child can chew well, offer her products which contain whole grains such as whole-wheat bread and homemade cereal bars.

FOOD	STAGE ONE: (APPROX. 4–6 MONTHS)	STAGE TWO: APPROX. 7–9 MONTHS	STAGE THREE: APPROX. 9–12 MONTHS	OVER 12 MONTHS
Vegetables	Purées of mild vegetables, e.g. parsnip, carrot, peas, cauliflower, spinach, zucchini, rutabaga, squash, sweet potato.	Try adding in tomatoes (peeled or strained to a pulp at first) and potato, in addition to, not in place of, other vegetables.	Introduce more strongly flavored vegetables, e.g. cabbage, leeks, onion, bell peppers.	Keep introducing new vegetables such as corn-on-the-cob, salad greens, halved cherry tomatoes, and revisit any that were rejected before.
Fruits	Purées of pear, cooked apple, banana, papaya, avocado, mango (all seeds and skins removed), apricots or plums that have been cooked and strained. Avoid citrus fruits and foods with lots of seeds such as raspberries.	Gradually offer other fruits, e.g. strawberries, kiwi fruit* (see page 25), orange, grapes. Make purées from soaked dried apricots and other dried fruits.	Add in canned fruits in natural juice.	Keep introducing new fruits and revisit any that were rejected before.
Dairy products	Avoid before 6 months.	Full-fat yogurt, cottage cheese, ricotta, mild cheddar, Monterey Jack cheese, or tofu. Whole milk used in small amounts for cooking and preparing foods*. Beware that most yogurts contain added sugar, which can cause tooth decay and encourage a sweet tooth, so don't give them too often. "Live culture" yogurts can be given to your baby after six months as long as the label doesn't say that the product isn't suitable for babies. Avoid blue or unpasteurized cheese.	Frozen yogurt (preferably homemade, see recipes pages 72 and 91) flavored with soft fruits such as banana, strawberries, mango, and puréed dried fruits. Avoid blue or unpasteurized cheese.	Ice cream. Keep introducing different types and flavors of cheese but continue to avoid blue or unpasteurized cheese.
Meat	Avoid before 6 months.	Purées of well-cooked lean red meat (including liver in small amounts once a week) and poultry. Avoid processed meats, e.g. bacon, sausages, salami, as they can be too salty.	Small amounts of unsmoked, low-salt ham. Low-fat, high meat content homemade meatballs, sausages, and burgers. Avoid processed meats, e.g. bacon, sausages, salami, as they can be too salty.	Storebought sausages, burgers etc. are fine occasionally but go for high meat content, low-fat, and low-salt varieties.

FOOD	STAGE ONE: (APPROX. 4–6 MONTHS)	STAGE TWO: APPROX. 7–9 MONTHS	STAGE THREE: APPROX. 9–12 MONTHS	OVER 12 MONTHS
Fish	Avoid before 6 months.	Once your baby is used to fruit and vegetables, you can start on steamed flounder, sole, or trout that is skinned and boned. Avoid shellfish.	Add in oily fish, e.g. fresh mackerel, salmon, tuna, plus canned fish, but make sure you remove all the bones. Avoid shellfish.	Shellfish* (see page 25). Small amounts of smoked fish. Avoid fish such as shark, swordfish, king mackerel, and tilefish as these may contain mercury which can affect the young nervous system.
Eggs	No.	Provided they are well cooked* (see page 25). Avoid raw or partially cooked eggs because of the risk of salmonella.	Provided they are well cooked* (see page 25).	Provided they are well cooked* (see page 25).
Nuts and seeds	No (see page 25).	Finely ground nuts and seeds (including peanuts) may be mixed in baby food from six months provided there is no history of family allergies (see page 25). Avoid whole/chopped nuts for risk of choking.	Finely ground nuts and seeds (including peanuts) may be mixed in baby food provided there is no history of family allergies (see page 25). Avoid whole/ chopped nuts for risk of choking.	Finely ground nuts and seeds (including peanuts) provided there is no history of family allergies (see page 25). Avoid whole/chopped nuts for risk of choking.
Honey	No. Honey can contain a type of bacteria which can produce toxins in the intestines causing serious illness (infant botulism).	No. Honey can contain a type of bacteria which can produce toxins in the intestines causing serious illness (infant botulism).	No. Honey can contain a type of bacteria which can produce toxins in the intestines causing serious illness (infant botulism).	Yes. After the age of one, the bacteria that can cause infant botulism are no longer a threat.

* Delay introducing these foods if there is a family history of allergy and seek professional advice from your pediatrician.

General tips

If your baby is too hungry she may become upset or frustrated so you may find it helpful to give her a little milk first before offering some solid foods.

If your child is having a "poor appetite day" don't be tempted to offer something like a cookie. Let her eat a bit less that day and she'll make up for it in the following days.

If your child didn't like cheese, try adding it into her diet in the form of a cheese sauce on lasagne. Research shows that a child often needs to be presented with a food several times before they'll accept it.

Sometimes babies object to the feel of a spoon in their mouths at first, so try feeding them by dipping your clean little finger in the food. Try altering the consistency, too.

As your baby's teeth come through, they can be cleaned gently with a small toothbrush and no paste. Use toothpaste containing fluoride as the teeth develop, but in babies and young children only very small amounts of toothpaste should be used to avoid excess fluoride ingestion.

Aim to feed your baby around the same times every day so that you can work toward establishing a mealtime routine.

when to introduce drinks

This chart is an approximate guide only. When you introduce drinks will depend a great deal on your baby's likes, dislikes, possible allergies, intolerances, appetite etc. If in doubt, speak to your pediatrician.

DRINKS	STAGE ONE: (APPROX. 4–6 MONTHS)	STAGE TWO: APPROX. 7–9 MONTHS	STAGE THREE: APPROX. 9–12 MONTHS	OVER 12 MONTHS
Milk	Breast or formula milk. Only give soy-based formulas on the advice of your doctor. Cows' milk, goat milk, sheep milk, and milks based on rice or oats are not suitable as a main drink until 12 months as they do not contain sufficient iron and other nutrients.	Breast or formula milk. Only give soy-based formulas on the advice of your doctor. Cows' milk, goat milk, sheep milk, and milks based on rice or oats are not suitable as a main drink until 12 months as they do not contain sufficient iron and other nutrients. Use them in small amounts for cooking.	Breast or formula milk. Only give soy-based formulas on the advice of your doctor. Cows' milk, goat milk, sheep milk, and milks based on rice or oats are not suitable as a main drink until 12 months as they do not contain sufficient iron and other nutrients. Use them in small amounts for cooking.	Whole cows', goat, and sheep milks can be given if pasteurized. Low-fat milk is only suitable as a drink if your child is over two years and has a varied diet. Skim milk is not suitable under five years as the calories from whole/low-fat milk are still needed.
Water	Fully breast-fed babies should not need any water until they start on solids. Babies fed on formula may need water in hot weather. Both tap water and bottled water must be boiled to sterilize it, then cooled. Some mineral waters have mineral contents unsuitable for babies. Look for the label "suitable for infant feeding."	Tap water no longer needs to be boiled. Some mineral waters have mineral contents unsuitable for babies. Look for the label "suitable for infant feeding." Mineral water still needs to be boiled at this stage.	Yes.	Yes.
Other drinks	No.	Avoid carbonated drinks, flavored milk, baby and herbal drinks, juice drinks, even those labeled "no added sugar" or "diet" as they may still be high in sugar, artificial flavorings, or sweeteners. Diluted fruit juices (1 part juice to 10 parts water) can now be given. Avoid tea or coffee (see Stage Three).	Continue to avoid the drinks mentioned in Stage Two. Diluted fruit juices (1 part juice to 10 parts water) are fine. Avoid tea and coffee; they reduce iron absorption in babies and small children, and if sugar is added, may contribute to tooth decay.	Avoid tea and coffee; they reduce iron absorption in babies and small children, and if sugar is added, may contribute to tooth decay.

family allergies

A very small number of children suffer from a food allergy but many grow out of it by the age of three. Children most at risk are those who have a family history of allergies, including eczema, asthma, or hay fever. Current guidelines recommend that children with a family history should be breast-fed for at least six months, longer if possible, as this helps to provide the child with protective antibodies.

There are a number of foods that are known to trigger allergies and intolerances in some susceptible children. The common allergenic foods include peanuts, nuts, milk, eggs, wheat, fish, and shellfish. These should never be fed to children under six months. If your child has a family history of allergies, introduce foods from the list above singly and make sure you observe him closely for several days—some symptoms occur immediately after eating while others may not present themselves for several hours, even days afterward. Introduce new foods at breakfast or lunchtime instead of in the evening so that if your baby does react to the food it does not happen during the night.

Common symptoms of a food allergy include sickness, diarrhea, bloating, coughing, wheezing, rashes (sometimes around the mouth), tingling of the mouth and throat, or eczema. If a family member suffers from food-related allergies or if you observe any of these symptoms after your child eats a certain food, consult your pediatrician. If necessary, she may refer you to a registered dietitian as the only way to accurately diagnose a food allergy is to eliminate suspected foods, wait for symptoms to disappear, and then slowly, after a period of time, reintroduce them one by one until symptoms reappear. This is called an "elimination diet" and requires careful supervision by a fully qualified professional, particularly where children are concerned, to prevent nutritional deficiencies occurring in their diet.

Allergy versus intolerance

A food allergy is when the immune system responds to a food by releasing antibodies, causing allergic symptoms such as those described before. It is thought that less than three per cent of the population has a true allergy to a food.

An intolerance, on the other hand, is when your child suffers from an ongoing problem, such as diarrhea or stomachache, which is systematically triggered by a certain food. One of the main differences between intolerance and allergy is that an intolerance doesn't involve the immune system and is generally not dangerous. Also, in the case of an intolerance, if your child doesn't eat the trigger food for a period of time he may then be able to tolerate it in moderation without any ill effects.

If you think your child may have a food allergy or intolerance, be sure to get a proper diagnosis from a health professional. Never be tempted to cut out major food groups such as wheat or dairy without seeking proper medical advice first, otherwise your child may miss out on essential nutrients and calories.

Cows' milk allergy

Approximately seven per cent of babies up to the age of 12 months suffer from an allergy to cows' milk. They usually grow out of it at an early age, but about one-fifth of all children diagnosed with a milk allergy remain allergic into adulthood.

The allergy is effected by casein and whey, allergens found in cows' milk. Children can be allergic to either whey or casein, or both. Those allergic to whey often find that they can tolerate pasteurized milk, since the heating process cancels the harmful effects of whey. However, heat treatment doesn't affect casein, so someone who is allergic to casein

Typical symptoms of lactose intolerance include bloating, diarrhea, and general abdominal discomfort. There is no medical treatment for this condition, but the symptoms can be avoided by controlling the amount of lactose in the diet. This is done by reducing or eliminating milk and foods made with milk from the diet. However, some children with lactose intolerance find that they can eat cheese and yogurt without suffering any unpleasant symptoms. This is because cheese contains much less lactose than milk. Yogurt contains a similar amount of lactose to milk but it is thought that the bacteria used to make it may aid its digestion.

If you suspect your baby has a lactose intolerance, talk to your pediatrician immediately and always seek her advice first before choosing a formula or switching to a different type of milk.

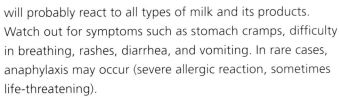

will probably react to all types of milk and its products. Watch out for symptoms such as stomach cramps, difficulty in breathing, rashes, diarrhea, and vomiting. In rare cases, anaphylaxis may occur (severe allergic reaction, sometimes life-threatening).

If you suspect your baby has a cows' milk allergy, talk to your pediatrician immediately and always seek her advice first before choosing a formula or switching to a different type of milk.

Lactose intolerance

Lactose intolerance is not the same as an allergy to cows' milk. An intolerance is caused by a shortage of the enzyme lactase, which is needed to break down lactose so it can be absorbed into the bloodstream. The shortage can occur because the person doesn't produce enough lactase. Sometimes, the production of lactase can be interrupted (often as a result of a stomach bug) so the intolerance only lasts for a short while.

Nuts

Tree nuts are not related to peanuts although many children who are allergic to peanuts are also allergic to other nuts.

Peanuts

It is estimated that one in 200 children may suffer from a peanut allergy, although the exact figure is unknown. Of all the foods, peanuts can cause the most serious reactions, the worst of which is anaphylactic shock, a rare but severe reaction in which the throat swells and breathing becomes restricted. It may be wise for women with a history of asthma, eczema, or food allergies to avoid peanuts and their products while pregnant and breast-feeding, and children with a family history of any allergies should avoid foods containing peanuts or their products until they are at least three. Recent research shows that up to a third of allergic children will outgrow their allergy by the age of seven.

If there is no history of family allergies, children can eat ground or crushed peanuts after six months. Never give whole nuts to children under five in case of choking.

Sesame seeds

A sesame allergy can cause severe reactions including anaphylaxis. People with a sesame allergy might also react to poppy seeds, kiwi fruit, hazelnuts, and rye. If a member of your family has a sesame allergy seek professional advice about the possibility of your child having it, and check food labels for sesame products.

Eggs

An egg allergy is mainly caused by proteins in egg whites. Children with egg allergies usually grow out of them by the age of five, during which time they become able to tolerate cooked egg, as cooking can break down and destroy some of the allergens in foods such as cakes.

Wheat-based foods containing gluten

Gluten is a type of protein found mainly in wheat, but also in barley, rye, and oats and therefore is present in foods such as bread, cereals, pasta, and cookies. The likelihood of developing an intolerance to gluten is greatly increased if it is given to babies at an early age (especially in children who have a family history of gluten intolerance) which is why it is recommended that foods containing gluten are never given to babies younger than six months and that the early stages of weaning only include nongluten foods such as rice or corn. Symptoms of gluten intolerance include a swollen abdomen, pale, foul-smelling stools, and loss of appetite. If someone in your family can't eat foods containing gluten, talk to your pediatrician before giving any wheat-, rye-, or barley-based foods to your baby.

Shellfish and fish

Fish allergy can often cause severe reactions. Children are less likely than adults to react to shellfish but can react to white fish. Cooking has very little effect upon fish allergens and if your child is diagnosed with a fish allergy, it is unlikely that he will grow out of it.

Soy

The symptoms of a soy allergy are similar to milk allergy and they include rashes, diarrhea, vomiting, stomach cramps, and breathing difficulties. Very rarely, soy can cause anaphylaxis. Soy allergy is common in childhood, however most children grow out of it by the age of two. Soy is used as an ingredient in lots of food products, including some baked goods, sweets, drinks, breakfast cereals, ice cream, margarine, pasta, and processed meats, so if a member of your family has a soy allergy always check food labels carefully. Never give soy infant formula to your baby without seeking professional advice first.

ensuring a healthy, balanced diet

Babies and children need lots of energy and nutrients. To make sure they get everything they need to develop into strong, healthy adults, it is important for them to eat a variety of foods from the groups below.

	GOOD SOURCES	NOT SO GOOD SOURCES	WHY ARE THEY NEEDED?
Carbohydrates	White and whole-grain bread, grains, cereals, rice, pasta, beans, potatoes, fruit, vegetables.	Cakes, cookies, chips, sweets, sugary cereals, preserves. These refined carbohydrates tend to be high in fat, salt, or sugar and low in nutrients.	Carbohydrates are energy providers. They are broken down by the body to form the body's main source of energy, glucose (blood sugar).
Protein	Meat, poultry, fish, eggs, milk, cheese, tofu, beans, grains, nuts.	Processed meats such as salami, sausages, and burgers can be high in saturated fats. Smoked or cured foods such as bacon, ham, and fish can also be high in salt.	Protein is essential for growth and development, cell maintenance and repair, and for the regulation of all body functions. It is made up of 22 individual "building blocks" called amino acids. Nonessential amino acids can be synthesized by the body. Essential amino acids must be provided by the diet. Animal sources of protein such as meat, poultry, dairy, fish, and eggs contain all the essential amino acids. Vegetable sources (with the exception of soybeans) don't, which is why (particularly for vegetarians) it is so important to eat a wide variety of foods. Only by combining proteins from beans, for example, with proteins from nuts or seeds can we obtain all the essential amino acids.
Fiber	Insoluble fiber (found in all plants): grains, particularly wheat, corn, rice, fruit, vegetables, beans. Soluble fiber: apples, oats, barley, rye, beans.	Unlike fats, carbohydrates, and protein, fiber does not provide any calories. It is however very filling, especially for very young children who have particularly small stomachs. Therefore, children under the age of two should not eat too many bulky, high-fiber foods such as whole grains, brown rice, whole-wheat pastas, bread etc.	Fiber is found in two main forms, soluble and insoluble. Most plant foods contain both but in varying proportions. Insoluble fiber, taken with sufficient fluids, increases stool bulk and speeds the passage of waste material through the bowels helping to decrease constipation and irritable bowel syndrome. Soluble fiber can help to reduce LDL ("bad" cholesterol) levels and control blood sugar levels, helping to reduce the risk of diabetes.

	GOOD SOURCES	NOT SO GOOD SOURCES	WHY ARE THEY NEEDED?
Fats	Oils such as olive, sunflower, corn, sesame. Omega-3 fatty acids: oily fish, e.g. trout, salmon, fresh (not canned) tuna, sardines, mackerel. Flaxseed, walnut, and canola oil, pumpkin, sunflower, and sesame seeds. Omega-3 enriched eggs. Omega-6 fatty acids: sunflower, grapeseed, safflower, walnut, corn, soy oils. Soft polyunsaturated margarines and walnuts.	Hydrogenated vegetable oil (trans fat) often found in commercially prepared margarine, cookies, cakes, ice cream, meat, hard margarine, butter, lard, cheese, processed meats such as sausages, burgers, salami.	Fats are a great source of energy, particularly in very young children who have relatively high energy requirements in relation to their small stomachs. This is why it is important not to give very young children reduced-fat foods. Fats are also needed for the healthy development of the brain, the nervous system (particularly omega-3 and omega-6 essential fatty acids), the hormonal, respiratory, and immune systems, as well as ensuring that beautiful, baby soft skin! Mono- and polyunsaturated fats lower cholesterol levels, helping to reduce the risk of heart disease. However, too many saturated and trans fats (unsaturated fats that have had their composition altered during the cooking and manufacturing process) can increase the risk of heart disease in later life.

cautionary advice on salt and sugar

Salt

Babies' kidneys are not able to process large amounts of salt. Keep salt levels to a minimum by making sure you never add extra salt to your baby's foods and avoid foods you know to contain a lot of salt such as bacon, smoked mackerel, fish canned in brine, and processed meats. Steer clear of any processed foods that aren't made specifically for babies too, such as pasta sauces and breakfast cereals, as these can also be high in salt and/or sugar.

Sugar

Do not add sugar in any form including malt, honey, and syrups to your baby's food as this will only encourage a sweet tooth and may lead to tooth decay when the first teeth start to come through. Honey can also contain a type of bacteria that may produce toxins in the intestines causing serious illness (infant botulism) in children under the age of one (see page 20). Instead, select fruits that are naturally ripe to sweeten baby food and only offer very diluted fruit juices (1 part juice to 10 parts water). Don't be tempted to give your baby a sugary snack like a cookie if she refuses to eat anything else—try some ripe berries or a juicy pear instead.

vitamins

It is important that your baby gets a variety of vitamins in his diet. This chart will tell you which foods are rich in the key vitamins and why they are beneficial to health.

VITAMIN TYPE	FOOD SOURCE	FUNCTION
Vitamin A	Liver, dairy produce, eggs, oily fish.	Promotes good vision, healthy eyes, skin, and growth.
Vitamin B_1	Whole grains, oatmeal, vegetables, dried yeast, liver, pork, nuts.	Plays an important role in releasing energy from food and ensures supply of glucose to the brain and nerves.
Vitamin B_2	Fortified breakfast cereals, dairy produce.	Promotes growth, healthy hair, skin, and nails and plays an important role in energy production and metabolizing carbohydrates, fats, and proteins.
Vitamin B_3	Yeast extract, meat, fish, liver.	Helps to release energy from food.
Vitamin B_6	Meat, fish, eggs, fortified breakfast cereals, whole grains, some vegetables.	Helps to metabolize protein and promotes good blood health.
Vitamin B_{12}	Meat, fish, animal products, seaweed.	Needed for the formation of blood cells and nerves.
Folate	Leafy greens, whole grains, nuts, beans, fortified breakfast cereals.	Vital for the formation of blood cells and infant development.
Vitamin C	Fruits, particularly citrus fruits and berries, vegetables.	Helps boost immune system, builds healthy bones, teeth, and connective tissue, heals wounds and enhances iron absorption.
Vitamin D	Fortified breakfast cereal, eggs, oily fish, fortified margarines and is manufactured by the body by sunlight on skin.	Needed for bone and teeth formation.
Vitamin E	Leafy green vegetables, seafood, poultry, egg yolks, whole grains, butter, nuts, seeds.	This antioxidant vitamin helps to boost the immune system, promote good heart health, protect against cancer, and ensure good, healthy skin.
Vitamin K	Yogurt, alfalfa, leafy green vegetables, milk, safflower oil, kelp, fish liver oils, egg yolks.	Essential for blood clotting.

minerals

It is important that your baby gets a variety of minerals in her diet. This chart will tell you which foods are rich in the key minerals and why they are beneficial to health.

MINERAL	FOOD SOURCES	FUNCTION
Calcium	Dairy products, soybeans, ground nuts and seeds, dried beans, leafy green vegetables, tofu, broccoli, fortified white bread. The softened bones in canned sardines and salmon contain calcium so mash the bones into the fish before serving.	Promotes strong bones and teeth and helps to control muscle/heart function and nervous system.
Iron	Liver, red meat, dark green leafy vegetables, beans, whole grains, nuts, seeds, dried fruit, fortified breakfast cereals.	Makes red blood cells, supplies oxygen to cells for energy and growth, and builds bones and teeth.
Zinc	Meat, dairy products, seeds, shellfish, nuts.	Essential for growth, development, and fertility. Also boosts immune system and assists with wound healing.
Selenium	Nuts (especially brazil nuts), seeds, beans, bread, fish, meat, eggs.	Antioxidant protecting against heart disease and cancer. Also helps promote normal growth, fertility, and metabolism.
Magnesium	Whole grains, nuts, seeds, leafy green vegetables.	Helps build strong bones and teeth, releases energy from food, and enhances nutrient absorption. Also promotes healthy heart.
Potassium	Fruit, vegetables, beans, nuts.	Works with sodium to regulate body fluids and is essential for correct functioning of cells, heart function, and blood pressure.
Iodine	Dairy products, seafood, seaweed.	Essential for correct functioning of thyroid gland, regulating oxygen uptake, and other vital body functions.

Remember that breast or formula milk should still be offered to your child as the main drink throughout the weaning process. He will continue to get vital nutrients from the milk while he starts on solids. He will usually drink approximately 16–20 ounces a day, although this amount will vary from child to child.

supplements

While it is always preferable to obtain the nutrients we need from foods rather than from supplements, the general consensus is that most children between the ages of six months and five years could benefit from taking drops containing vitamins A, C, and D. This is particularly appropriate if they don't eat meat or oily fish, or if their skin doesn't get exposed to daylight very often (either because they spend a lot of time indoors or because they always wear clothes that cover almost all of their skin when they are outdoors). This is because the body needs sunlight on the skin to enable it to make vitamin D (which is vital for the formation of strong, healthy bones).

Children who have a good appetite and eat a wide variety of foods, including fruit and vegetables, might not need vitamin drops and babies receiving infant formula every day do not generally require drops as the vitamins are already added to the formula.

vegetarian and vegan babies

Vegetarianism

The principles of weaning are the same for vegetarian babies as for nonvegetarian babies. However, it is essential to ensure that any nutrients potentially lost from a child's diet by taking out meat, fish, or dairy are replaced with other foods (see chart on pages 26–27). Nonvegetarian children get much of their iron from meat. For vegetarian babies over six months this can be found in soaked and puréed dried apricots, small amounts of prune juice, red lentils, mixed grains, and iron-fortified baby breakfast cereals. Vitamin C helps to enhance iron absorption, so serving vitamin C-rich foods at the same time as iron-rich foods, for example cooked tomatoes with red lentils, or dried apricots puréed with a little fresh orange juice, can be a good idea (see page 30 for more good sources of iron and page 29 for sources of vitamin C). Also, try offering diluted citrus fruit juices with your child's meal.

A vegetarian diet can be high in fiber and therefore more bulky and filling, so make sure your child gets enough energy in her diet by giving smaller, more frequent main meals throughout the day, plus one or two snacks. Include plenty of dairy products too, such as cheese, yogurt, and milk for vitamin D and calcium. Speak to your pediatrician about the possible need for extra supplements.

Veganism

With appropriate care, varied vegan diets can provide all the nutrients a baby needs for growth and development. However, such diets can be high in fiber which can result in low energy intake and interfere with absorption of minerals such as iron, zinc, and copper. If your child does have a vegan diet it is important to work closely with your doctor who may refer you to a registered pediatric dietitian to ensure that your child's diet has all the nutrients it needs.

a note about organic foods

Children deserve the best possible food made from the safest, healthiest ingredients. Today, going organic implies buying the most nutritious foods. But the debate about the health benefits of organic food rages on. There is little evidence to show that crops grown organically have a better nutrient content than those produced nonorganically. However, not enough research has been conducted in this area and the existing studies are believed to be out of date or based on inadequate methods. All of which can leave us parents unsure about whether to buy organic for our children.

The most important factor in the health of your children is that they eat plenty of fruit and vegetables. Research shows time and time again that a diet rich in brightly colored fruit and vegetables is key to ensuring good health both now and in the future, so if paying more for your fruit and vegetables means having to buy less, forget it. If, however, organic food, especially fruit, vegetables, meat, and dairy, are easily available and finances allow, do buy them. Children's cells are multiplying at their peak as their bodies grow but their kidneys are immature and therefore less able to filter out and break down harmful substances. And their nervous systems are rapidly developing—something that can be disrupted by exposure to toxins. Weight for weight, children (particularly babies) consume higher proportions of fruit and vegetables than adults so even small levels of pesticides can add up.

Apart from anything else, organic foods do not contain genetically modified ingredients, flavorings, or colorings. Moreover, organic animals have not been routinely given the hormones and antibiotics that nonorganic animals are reared on, therefore their residues will not be found in the meat. Finally, organic food production is far kinder to animals and the environment, so buying organic means we are helping our children to inherit a far healthier world to live in.

6–9 months

purées

gentle lentil purée

Makes approx. 20 cubes

1 teaspoon extra virgin olive oil
1 small carrot, peeled and finely chopped
1 celery rib, finely chopped
¼ cup red lentils, washed
a little of your baby's usual milk, to thin

Lentils really are one of nature's superfoods. They are full of energy, fiber, and they are also a good source of iron.

Heat the olive oil in a heavy saucepan, then add the carrot and celery and sauté for about 10 minutes, or until soft. Add the red lentils and 1¼ cups water and cook gently for a further 15 minutes, or until the lentils are soft. Purée to the desired consistency with a handheld blender, adding a little extra water or your baby's usual milk if it is too thick. Serve, or spoon into ice cube trays, let cool, and freeze.

baked sweet potato purée

Makes approx. 30–40 cubes

2 large sweet potatoes, washed and scrubbed
1 tablespoon extra virgin olive oil
a little of your baby's usual milk, to thin

Baking is a great way to cook vegetables without losing any of their valuable vitamins and minerals. You really could not find an easier recipe than this.

Preheat the oven to 400°F. Prick the potatoes all over with a fork. Rub the olive oil all over the potatoes, then bake in the preheated oven for 1½–2 hours, depending on the size of the potato. The cooked potatoes should be crispy on the outside and give a little when squeezed. Cut in half, scoop out the flesh into a bowl, and mash. Add a little extra water or your baby's usual milk if it is too thick. Serve, or spoon into ice cube trays, let cool, and freeze.

brown rice purée

Makes approx. 30 cubes

¾ cup brown rice, washed under cold water

Keep a few frozen cubes of this purée as it can be eaten on its own or used to bulk out both savory and sweet dishes, such as apricot or prune purée.

Cook the rice according to the manufacturer's instructions. Drain and purée with a handheld blender. Serve, or spoon into ice cube trays, let cool, and freeze.

broccoli purée

Makes approx. 20 cubes

16 oz. broccoli, chopped
a little of your baby's usual milk, to thin (optional)

I have used broccoli here because it is a good source of vitamin C, iron, and calcium—vital nutrients for very small babies—but this extremely simple purée would work just as well with carrots, butternut squash, parsnips, or cauliflower.

Steam the broccoli or simmer in a pan with a little water for about 10–15 minutes until soft throughout. Remove from the steamer or pan, but reserve the cooking liquid. Purée to the desired consistency with a handheld blender, adding a little cooking liquid or your baby's usual milk if it is too thick. Serve, or spoon into ice cube trays, let cool, and freeze.

easy-does-it root vegetable purée

Makes approx. 20 cubes

1 medium sweet potato, peeled and chopped
5 carrots, peeled and chopped
2–3 parsnips, peeled and chopped
a little of your baby's usual milk, to thin (optional)

Root vegetables are easy on the stomach, packed with nutrients, and automatically cook up to a great consistency for purées.

Steam the potato, carrots, and parsnips or simmer them in a pan with a little water for about 20 minutes, or until cooked. Remove from the steamer or pan, but reserve the cooking liquid. Purée to the desired consistency with a handheld blender, adding a little cooking liquid or your baby's usual milk if it is too thick. Serve, or spoon into ice cube trays, let cool, and freeze.

flounder purée

Makes approx. 20 cubes

⅓ cup brown rice, washed under cold water
3½ oz. flounder fillet, skinned and boned
a few fresh parsley leaves
a little of your baby's usual milk, to thin

It's best to offer this to babies only once they are used to eating purées, so avoid serving before 7 months. As your baby progresses, do add steamed vegetables.

Boil the rice according to the manufacturer's instructions, drain, and set aside. Meanwhile, gently steam the fish for approximately 10 minutes. Sprinkle with the parsley and steam for a further 2 minutes. Purée the rice, fish, and parsley with a little of your baby's usual milk to the required consistency. Serve, or spoon into ice cube trays, let cool, and freeze.

perfectly peachy purée

Makes 1–2 portions

**1 small, ripe peach, pitted, peeled, and chopped
a little rice cereal, to thicken**

Make sure you use a ripe peach for this recipe—not only does it taste better, it is gentler on your baby's stomach too. This particular purée is best eaten fresh, so avoid freezing and thawing.

Purée the peach flesh with a handheld blender or mash with a fork. Stir in a little rice cereal if it is too thin. Serve.

apricot and mango purée

Makes 1–2 portions

**2 large fresh apricots, pitted, peeled, and chopped
½ ripe mango, pitted, peeled, and chopped
a little rice cereal, to thicken**

This little duo is rich in beta carotene, the plant form of vitamin A, which helps to ensure good vision and boosts the immune system. Add banana for a more filling purée. Again, this purée is best eaten fresh, so avoid freezing and thawing.

Purée the apricots and mango with a handheld blender or mash with a fork. Stir in a little rice cereal if it is too thin. Serve.

melon purée

Makes 1 portion

**½ small cantaloupe melon, seeded
1–2 slices of banana, mashed, or 1–2 teaspoons rice cereal, to thicken**

This is a lovely gentle purée that is mild in taste and ideal for the very early stages of weaning. Particularly ripe melon may result in a runny consistency so expect to add a pinch or two of rice cereal or some banana to thicken the purée.

Scoop out the flesh from the melon and purée with a handheld blender. Stir in some mashed banana or rice cereal to thicken. Serve immediately.

avocado and papaya purée

Makes 1 portion

¼ small avocado, pitted, peeled, and chopped
½ small papaya, seeded, peeled, and chopped
1–2 tablespoons your baby's usual milk

Avocados and papayas are both extremely easy on the digestive system, making this a great purée if your baby seems to be a bit off her food but still needs a nutritious snack.

Put the avocado, papaya, and milk in a bowl and mash or purée with a handheld blender. Serve immediately.

apple purée

Makes 6–8 portions

4 sweet apples, peeled, cored, and chopped
¼ cup unsweetened apple juice or water

This works just as well with pears. Alternatively, just swap 2 apples for 2 ripe pears and you can combine them in the same recipe. As your baby progresses, add a little full-fat yogurt and a pinch of ground cinnamon.

Put the apples, apple juice, and 2 tablespoons water in a saucepan and cook over low heat for 8 minutes, or until tender. Blend the fruit to a smooth purée, let cool a little, then serve.

apple and apricot purée

Makes 1–2 portions

½ apple, peeled, cored, and chopped
3 dried apricots, chopped
1 teaspoon rice cereal
1 tablespoon your baby's usual milk

A baby is born with all the iron he needs to get him through his first 5 or 6 months. Then iron stores need to be replenished by his diet. Dried apricots are a good source of iron and their sweetness blends beautifully with puréed apple.

Put the apple, dried apricots, and 2 tablespoons water in a small saucepan and cook for 5–8 minutes until the fruit is soft. Purée with a handheld blender until smooth. Mix the rice cereal with the milk and stir into the purée to thicken. Serve immediately.

avocado purée

Makes 1 portion

½ ripe avocado, pitted, peeled,
  and chopped
a little of your baby's usual milk,
  to thin

Avocados contain more nutrients than any other fruit (avocados are fruit, not vegetables!). They are a good source of protein and monounsaturated fats, and are high in calories, which makes them ideal for growing babies.

Mash the avocado with the back of a fork, adding a little of your baby's usual milk if it's too thick. Serve immediately before the purée turns brown.

papaya purée

Makes 1 portion

1 ripe papaya, seeded, peeled,
  and chopped

Papayas are full of fiber, vitamins A and C (powerful immune-boosting antioxidants), potassium, which helps to regulate fluid levels within the body, and folate, vital for the proper development of infants.

Mash the papaya flesh with the back of a fork until smooth. Serve.

banana and mango purée

Makes 1 portion

1 small ripe banana
1 slice of ripe mango
a little of your baby's usual
  milk or a pinch of rice cereal,
  to purée

Bananas and mangoes both contain fiber, vitamin B_6, which helps to make red blood cells, and vitamin C. Bananas are also a good source of energy and potassium.

Peel and chop the banana and purée it with the mango using a handheld blender until smooth. Add a little of your baby's usual milk if it's too thick or a pinch or two of rice cereal if it's too thin.

more fingerfood ideas (from 7 months)

- Lightly cooked carrot sticks, broccoli florets, and large pasta pieces
- Unsalted rice cakes
- Cold cucumber sticks can be very soothing on sore, teething gums so take the cucumber straight from the fridge and cut sticks 2 inches long and ½ inch thick.

super-quick fingerfoods

From 6 months, you can start giving your baby fingerfoods—healthy snacks they can pick up and eat themselves. This encourages them to chew, and teaches them how to feed themselves. It also adds a little interest and variety to mealtimes and helps your child to develop coordination skills as they practice getting food from table to mouth.

roast parsnips

Makes 1 portion

1 parsnip, peeled and quartered lengthwise (use more parsnips if you want to make purée too, see recipe)
3 tablespoons extra virgin olive oil

Preheat the oven to 400°F. Put the olive oil in a roasting pan and heat in the oven.

Steam or boil the parsnips until nearly tender. Remove the parsnips you wish to use as fingerfood. Leave any remaining parsnips for the purée in the pan and continue to cook for 5 minutes, or until fully tender. Purée with handheld blender or mash with a fork, then serve, or spoon into ice cube trays, let cool, and freeze.

Remove the roasting pan from the oven and toss the parsnip quarters in the hot oil. Roast for 30–40 minutes until crisp and golden, basting halfway through. Let cool before serving.

cinnamon eggy bread fingers

Makes 1 portion

1 egg
½ teaspoon ground cinnamon
1 slice of white or whole-grain bread, cut into narrow fingers
½ tablespoon extra virgin olive oil

Break the egg into a shallow dish. Add the cinnamon and beat well with a fork. Turn the bread fingers in the egg mixture until they are thoroughly coated, then let them sit in the mixture for a few minutes to soak up the egg.

Heat the olive oil in a skillet over medium heat. Once the oil is hot, put the eggy bread fingers in the skillet. After about a minute, the slices should be golden brown underneath, so flip them over and cook the other side. Put them on a warm plate to cool slightly before serving.

main meals

Lamb and beef are both great sources of iron, and combined with a few well chosen vegetables they can make a truly delicious and comforting main meal for your little one.

lamb and barley hotpot

Makes 4–6 portions

5 oz. lean ground lamb
⅓ cup pearl barley
1 small onion, peeled and chopped
1 carrot, peeled and chopped
¼ cup chopped red bell pepper
1 small garlic clove, crushed
1 tablespoon tomato paste

Put the lamb, pearl barley, onion, carrot, bell pepper, garlic, and tomato paste in a large saucepan. Cover with water, stir well, breaking up the lamb, and simmer for 45 minutes, stirring from time to time and adding more water if it dries out.

Let cool slightly, then purée with a handheld blender to the desired consistency.

Note: Barley is not recommended for babies under 6 months and ideally, first tastes should consist of nonwheat cereals and low-fiber grains such as plain rice cereal, homemade rice purées, and oats. A small amount of barley, after 7 months, and in combination with other ingredients, is fine.

slow-cooked beef, leek, and sweet potato casserole

Makes 4–6 portions

2 tablespoons unsalted butter
1 leek, white part only, sliced
5 oz. lean beef stewing meat, cubed
1 small sweet potato, peeled and chopped
1⅔ cups low-sodium beef broth

Preheat the oven to 350°F.

Melt the butter in a heavy saucepan and sauté the leek for 5 minutes, or until softened. Add the beef and sauté until brown. Add the potato and broth and bring to a boil.

Transfer the contents of the pan to a casserole dish and bake in the preheated oven for 1½–2 hours, or until the meat is tender. Purée with a handheld blender to the desired consistency.

Chicken is a great source of lean protein and because it is quite mild in flavor it combines well with a whole host of ingredients, from butter beans right through to apple and couscous. Whenever possible, buy organic chicken (see page 33). It is more expensive than nonorganic but the quality of the meat is far superior.

chicken and apple couscous

Makes 4–6 portions

2 small skinless chicken breasts, chopped
2 small red apples, peeled, cored, and sliced
2 cups unsweetened apple juice
2 tablespoons cooked couscous

Put the chicken, apples, and apple juice in a saucepan and simmer gently for about 10 minutes or until the chicken is cooked right through.

Remove from heat and put the contents of the saucepan in a food processor with the couscous. Blend to a purée and serve immediately.

creamy chicken and butter beans

Makes 4–6 portions

2 teaspoons extra virgin olive oil
2 carrots, peeled and chopped
2 celery ribs, chopped
1 small onion
3 tablespoons canned butter beans
3½ oz. cooked chicken, chopped
1 teaspoon chopped fresh parsley
1 cup low-sodium chicken broth
1 tablespoon cream

Heat the olive oil in a heavy saucepan, then sauté the carrots, celery, and onion for a few minutes until the vegetables have softened slightly.

Add the butter beans, chicken, parsley, and broth and simmer for 20 minutes, or until the vegetables are cooked through.

Stir in the cream and purée with a handheld blender to the desired consistency.

mariner's cheesy parsley mash

Makes 4–6 portions

5 oz. potatoes, peeled and
   chopped
5 oz. haddock or cod fillet,
   skinned and boned
3 peppercorns
1 bay leaf
a sprig of fresh parsley, chopped
6 tablespoons your baby's usual
   milk
½ cup grated mild cheddar
2 tablespoons unsalted butter
freshly grated nutmeg

Put the potatoes in a saucepan of boiling water and cook for about 20 minutes, or until soft. Meanwhile, put the fish in another pan with the peppercorns, bay leaf, and parsley. Pour the milk over and poach the fish for about 5 minutes.

Remove the fish from the milk with a slotted spoon. Discard the peppercorns and bay leaf and reserve the milk.

Drain the potatoes and put them in a food processor with the poached fish, cheddar, butter, a little nutmeg, and the reserved milk. Process to the desired consistency, adding more milk if it's too thick.

vegetable goulash

Makes 4–6 portions

2 tablespoons unsalted butter
½ leek, thinly sliced
9 oz. potatoes, peeled and
   chopped
½ cup frozen peas
2½ oz. baby spinach, tough
   stalks removed (or frozen
   spinach, thawed)
1½ oz. broccoli, chopped into
   small florets

Melt the butter in a saucepan and sauté the leeks for 2–3 minutes, or until softened, then add the potatoes. Pour ¾ cup water over, bring to a boil, then cover with a lid and simmer for 7–8 minutes.

Add the peas, spinach, and broccoli and cook for 3–4 minutes.

Put everything in a blender and purée to the desired consistency, adding a little extra water or your baby's usual milk if necessary.

Variation: Stir in a little grated cheddar, cottage cheese, or a spoonful of cream.

Many people forget about the possibility of using fresh herbs when cooking for babies. Use them in small, baby-friendly quantities and they really can enhance the flavor of a dish. Here are some comforting, tasty recipes for your baby to try, all packed full of fresh, nutrient-rich vegetables. And there are some fragrant herbs for your baby to try too, such as parsley, mint, and bay leaves.

minty mushy peas and potatoes

Makes 4–6 portions

1 tablespoon unsalted butter
1 small onion, finely chopped
1 small zucchini, thinly sliced
8 oz. potatoes, peeled and chopped
¾ cup low-sodium vegetable or chicken broth
1 cup frozen peas
2–3 fresh mint leaves, chopped

Melt the butter in a saucepan and sauté the onion for about 3 minutes, or until softened. Add the zucchini and sauté for 1 minute.

Add the potatoes, pour over the broth, then cover with a lid and simmer for 10–15 minutes.

Add the frozen peas and mint, bring to a boil, then reduce the heat and continue to cook for 3 minutes.

Put everything in a blender and purée to the desired consistency.

sweets

Berries, packed full of immune-boosting vitamin C and disease-fighting antioxidants, really are one of life's superfoods and they taste delicious too, especially when they are combined with creamy yogurt.

Makes 1–2 portions

½ cup frozen mixed berries
1 ripe peach, pitted, peeled, and chopped
1 fresh mint leaf, chopped
1 tablespoon plain yogurt

berry berry peachy purée

Put the mixed berries, peach, and mint in a saucepan and simmer for about 5 minutes, or until the berries have thawed and collapsed a little. Let cool slightly, then press through a strainer into a bowl and stir in the yogurt.

Makes 1–2 portions

2 ripe pears, peeled, cored, and chopped
¾ cup blueberries
1 tablespoon unsweetened apple juice
2 tablespoons rice cereal

blueberry and pear pudding

Put the pears, blueberries, and apple juice in a heavy saucepan, cover with a lid, and cook over low heat for about 5 minutes.

Put the contents of the saucepan in a blender and purée to the desired consistency. Stir in the rice cereal.

These recipes all combine deliciously tasty fruits, such as apples, cherries, and plums, with something a little more substantial such as oats, banana, or semolina to fill hungry tummies—perfect as desserts or even a healthy breakfast to start the day.

little cherub's cherry semolina

Makes 1–2 portions

6 sweet cherries, pitted
1 tablespoon unsweetened apple juice
1 ripe banana
1 tablespoon semolina

Put the cherries and apple juice in a small saucepan and simmer for 2 minutes.

Peel and mash the banana, add it to the pan, and simmer for just under 1 minute.

Stir in the semolina and serve, or purée to the desired consistency using a handheld blender.

apricot, apple, and oat dessert

Makes 2 portions

3 dried apricots
1 apple, peeled, cored, and chopped
⅔ cup your baby's usual milk
2 tablespoons rolled oats

Put the apricots and apple in a saucepan with 4 tablespoons water and cook over medium heat for 5 minutes.

Meanwhile, put the milk and oats in another pan, bring to a boil, and simmer, stirring constantly for 4–5 minutes until thickened.

Put the contents of both pans in a blender and purée to the desired consistency, adding a little more milk if necessary.

plum pudding

Makes 1–2 portions

2 large plums, pitted, peeled, and chopped
1 ripe banana

Steam the plums until tender.

Peel and chop the banana, add it to the plums, then purée to the desired consistency using a handheld blender. Serve immediately.

9–12 months

purées

strawberries and greek yogurt

Choose ripe strawberries here, full of natural sugars, to complement the rich, creamy Greek yogurt. Your baby will gobble this purée up in no time!

Makes 1–2 portions

6–10 ripe strawberries, hulled and halved
2 tablespoons Greek yogurt

Mash or purée the strawberries with a handheld blender and stir in the yogurt. Serve immediately.

blueberry and banana purée

Makes 1 portion

1 ripe banana
1 tablespoon ripe blueberries

Ounce for ounce, blueberries have the highest antioxidant capacity of any fruit, helping to strengthen the immune system and protect against cancer. Out of season, they can be tart so this is better made at their peak in the summer.

Peel the banana, put it with the blueberries in a bowl, and mash or purée with a handheld blender. Serve immediately.

pear and cottage cheese purée

Makes 1 portion

1 ripe, juicy pear, peeled, cored, and chopped
1 tablespoon cottage cheese

Cottage cheese is a great source of calcium and protein and it works naturally well with a ripe, juicy pear.

Put the pear and cottage cheese in a bowl and mash or purée with a handheld blender. Serve immediately.

super-quick fingerfoods

The white flour and cheese in these cheese straws both contain calcium. The straws are popular with older children too, so keep the recipe handy for when hunger strikes. Dunk them in Ripe Tomato Salsa (see page 88).

cheese straws

Makes about 20 straws

Ripe Tomato Salsa (page 88)
5 tablespoons whole-wheat
    flour
5 tablespoons all-purpose flour
½ cup finely grated Parmesan
¾ cup finely grated mild cheddar
a pinch of cayenne pepper
6½ tablespoons unsalted butter,
    cubed
1 egg yolk

Preheat the oven to 400°F. Lightly grease a large baking sheet and cover it with baking parchment.

Combine the whole-wheat and all-purpose flours, Parmesan, cheddar, and cayenne pepper in a large mixing bowl and rub in the butter until the mixture resembles fine bread crumbs. Add the egg yolk and mix until the dough comes together.

Roll out the dough on a lightly floured surface until you have a square about ¼ inch thick. Cut into long strips or straws and place on the prepared baking sheet, leaving a small space between each straw. Bake in the preheated oven for 8–12 minutes, until golden.

Remove from the oven and transfer to a wire rack to cool. Store in an airtight container for 3–4 days. Serve with Ripe Tomato Salsa.

Variation: Add a heaping teaspoon of dried mixed herbs to the flour.

oatcakes

Makes 10–15 oatcakes

1¾ cups oat flour,
    plus extra to dust
a pinch of baking soda
1 tablespoon sunflower oil
6 tablespoons boiling water

Preheat the oven to 350°F.

Combine the oat flour and baking soda in a bowl. Gradually add the oil and water and stir to make a stiff dough. Leave for a few minutes to swell.

Roll out the dough thinly on a surface dusted with oat flour and cut into fingers. Place on a baking sheet and bake for 25 minutes—check occasionally to make sure they aren't burning.

Remove from the oven and transfer to a wire rack to cool. Store in an airtight container for 3–4 days. Serve buttered.

main meals

Wham, Bam, Lamb really is the easiest, tastiest meal to prepare. However, the longer it cooks, the better it gets, so make it well in advance, pop it in the oven, and forget about it for a while. The Beefed-up Bolognese contains loads of vegetables so it's full of vitamins, minerals, and fiber and the ground beef is a great source of iron, too.

wham, bam, lamb!

Makes 6–8 portions

about 8 oz. lamb cutlets
6 oz. potatoes, peeled and diced
3 carrots, peeled and sliced
1 small leek, finely chopped
1 small onion, peeled and
   chopped
2 tomatoes, peeled, seeded,
   and chopped
⅔ cup low-sodium lamb or
   beef broth

Preheat the oven to 350°F.

Put the lamb, potatoes, carrots, leek, onion, tomatoes, and broth in a small casserole dish, cover with a lid, and cook in the preheated oven for 1–1½ hours until the lamb is tender.

For older children, simply chop into small pieces and serve. For little ones between nine and 12 months, purée with a handheld blender or in a food processor first.

beefed-up bolognese

Makes 6–8 portions

1 tablespoon vegetable oil
½ small onion, chopped
1 small garlic clove, crushed
1 celery rib, finely chopped
1 carrot, peeled and grated
¼ eggplant, diced
4 oz. lean ground beef
½ teaspoon tomato paste
1 teaspoon dried mixed herbs
a 14-oz. can chopped tomatoes
2 teaspoons red wine vinegar
1½ oz. spaghetti

Heat the vegetable oil in saucepan, then sauté the onion, garlic, and celery for 4 minutes.

Add the carrot and eggplant and cook for 2 minutes. Add the beef and stir until brown. Stir in the tomato paste, herbs, canned tomatoes, and red wine vinegar.

Bring the mixture to a boil. Reduce the heat, cover, and cook for about 10 minutes.

Transfer the bolognese to a food processor and blend for a few seconds to give it a slightly smoother texture. Cook the spaghetti in lightly salted boiling water according to the manufacturer's instructions. Drain and chop into small pieces.

Mix the spaghetti into the bolognese and serve.

Salmon, along with other oily fish such as trout, fresh tuna, mackerel, and sardines, contains essential fatty acids that have been shown to enhance brain development, lower the risk of heart disease, and strengthen the immune system. Sweet potatoes and broccoli are both great sources of vitamins A and C and are particularly rich in compounds that protect against cancer and many other diseases.

salmon, sweet potato, and broccoli chowder

Makes 10–12 portions

3 tablespoons unsalted butter
1 large onion, chopped
¾ cup all-purpose flour
3 cups low-sodium chicken broth
1 cup whole milk (or your baby's usual milk)
1 large sweet potato, peeled and diced
1 bay leaf
1 teaspoon fresh thyme leaves
16 oz. skinned salmon fillet, cubed
1 small broccoli stalk, chopped

Melt the butter in a large, heavy saucepan, then fry the onion for about 5 minutes, or until softened. Add the flour and stir until smooth. Beat in the broth and milk, then add the sweet potato, bay leaf, and thyme. Bring to a boil, reduce the heat, and simmer gently, stirring occasionally, for 8 minutes.

Add the salmon and broccoli and simmer for a further 5 minutes.

Mash or blend with a handheld blender to the desired consistency.

cheatin' zucchini cheddar chicken

Makes 1–2 portions

1 zucchini, sliced
1 oz. cooked chicken, chopped
¼ cup grated mild cheddar
1 tablespoon cream
a little of your baby's usual milk, to thin

Steam or microwave the zucchini until tender.

Put the chicken, cheddar, cream, and zucchini in a saucepan.

Heat until piping hot. Purée with a handheld blender to the desired consistency, adding a splash of milk if required. Let cool a little, then serve.

creamy tomato and basil pasta

Makes 6–8 portions

2 oz. penne
2 tablespoons extra virgin
    olive oil
1 onion, finely chopped
1 garlic clove, crushed
20 oz. chopped canned
    tomatoes
1 tablespoon tomato paste
1 tablespoon balsamic vinegar
1 teaspoon sugar
2 tablespoons mascarpone
    cheese
1 tablespoon finely chopped
    fresh basil

Cook the penne in lightly salted boiling water according to the manufacturer's instructions. Meanwhile, heat the olive oil in a saucepan, then add the onion and garlic and sauté for about 5 minutes, or until softened.

Add the tomatoes, tomato paste, vinegar, and sugar and cook uncovered over medium heat for about 12 minutes. Add the mascarpone cheese and stir until melted.

Finally, stir in the basil.

Drain the pasta and cut it up or mash it into small pieces for babies, or leave whole for older children and adults. Pour the sauce over and serve.

four veg, ham, and cheese bake

Makes 6–8 portions

3 tablespoons unsalted butter
1 small leek, thinly sliced
4 carrots, peeled and very finely
    chopped
2 oz. broccoli, chopped
½ cup fresh or frozen peas
1 tablespoon flour
⅔ cup whole milk
a sprig of fresh parsley, finely
    chopped
¾ cup grated mild cheddar
5 oz. unsmoked cooked ham,
    finely chopped

Melt 1 tablespoon of the butter in saucepan, then sauté the leek for 2–3 minutes. Add the carrots, cover with water, and cook for 10 minutes. Stir in the broccoli and peas and cook for a further 5 minutes or until the vegetables are tender.

Preheat the broiler to hot.

Meanwhile, melt the remaining butter in a separate saucepan, stir in the flour, and cook for 1 minute. Gradually beat in the milk. Stir in the parsley and bring the sauce to a boil, stirring until it has thickened. Remove from the heat, add two-thirds of the cheddar, and stir until melted.

Drain the vegetables and mix them with the ham and sauce in an ovenproof dish. Sprinkle the top with the remaining cheese and put under the hot broiler for a few minutes until the cheese has melted. Let cool slightly, then serve as is, provided you have chopped the vegetables small enough. Alternatively, mash or purée to the desired consistency.

The whole family will love both of these recipes so they are ideal for those busy days when you simply don't have time to cook twice. The sauce from the bake is also good for older children and adults as a filling for baked potatoes or savory pancakes, so it's a useful recipe to have on standby.

This ratatouille makes such a versatile sauce you can use it over pasta, potatoes, or rice. You can also try adding flaked canned tuna or fresh mackerel to it. Instead of the usual mashed potato, try this nutrient-packed alternative made with fresh vegetables, steamed to retain their goodness, and mashed with a little cashew butter. Cashew nuts contain protein, fiber, potassium, B vitamins, folate, and magnesium—bursting with health!

easy ratatouille sauce and couscous

Makes 6–8 portions

1 large green bell pepper,
   seeded and diced
a 14-oz. can chopped tomatoes
1 large zucchini, diced
1 eggplant, diced
1 onion, peeled and thinly sliced
1 carrot, peeled and diced
1 celery rib, diced
1 garlic clove, crushed
1 bay leaf
1 tablespoon finely chopped
   fresh basil
6–8 tablespoons freshly
   cooked couscous

Put the bell pepper, tomatoes, zucchini, eggplant, onion, carrot, celery, garlic, and bay leaf in a large saucepan and bring to a boil. Skim off any sediment.

Cover and simmer for about 20 minutes, or until all the vegetables are tender and most of the liquid has evaporated. If there is too much liquid, remove the lid and boil briskly for a few minutes to burn off some of the liquid.

Remove the bay leaf and stir in the basil. Let cool slightly, then serve as is with some couscous, provided you have chopped the vegetables small enough. Alternatively, mash or purée to the desired consistency.

cashew buttered vegetable mash

Makes 1–2 portions

2 broccoli florets
1 small carrot, peeled and
   chopped
1 small potato, peeled and
   chopped
1 tablespoon corn kernels
3 oz. unsalted cashews
a drizzle of extra virgin olive oil

Steam the broccoli, carrot, potato, and corn until soft.

Meanwhile, put the cashews and a drizzle of olive oil in a food processor and whizz until you get a smooth butter.

Drain the vegetables and mash or purée to the desired consistency using a little water from the bottom of the pan or steamer if necessary. Stir in 1–2 teaspoons of the cashew butter.

Serve it just as it is as an entrée for your little one aged nine to 12 months, or as a side dish for older children and adults to accompany fish or meat.

Note: Only serve this if you are sure your child is not allergic to nuts (see page 25).

sweets

Fresh fruits always make delicious, healthy desserts, but even babies can get fed up of the usual puréed apples and pears, so here are three slightly different ways to serve up fruits for dessert.

tropical mixed fruits

Makes 4 portions

½ mango, pitted and peeled
½ papaya, seeded and peeled
1 kiwi fruit, peeled
1 small banana
fresh juice of ½ orange

Finely chop all the fruit and combine with the orange juice.

Serve as is if the pieces are small enough, or mash to the desired consistency for young babies.

fall fruits with cinnamon

Makes 1–2 portions

1 sweet apple, peeled, cored, and chopped
1 ripe pear, peeled, cored, and chopped
1 ripe plum, pitted, peeled, and chopped
2 tablespoons unsweetened apple juice
a pinch of ground cinnamon

Put the apple, pear, plum, apple juice, and cinnamon in a saucepan and bring to a boil.

Turn down the heat and simmer for approximately 5 minutes, or until tender.

Remove from the heat and mash or purée to the desired consistency. Let cool slightly before serving.

mango and orange frozen yogurt

Makes 4–6 portions

1 ripe mango, pitted, peeled, and chopped
2 large unwaxed oranges, peeled and chopped, plus 1 teaspoon finely grated peel
2 tablespoons plain yogurt
1 tablespoon cream

Put the mango, orange, orange peel, yogurt, and cream in a blender and process until smooth.

Pour the mixture into individual freezerproof containers or ice cube trays and freeze for 3 hours, stirring occasionally to break up any ice crystals.

Transfer to the refrigerator to soften for 30 minutes before serving.

I love these recipes as they are super healthy and yet comforting at the same time. Not only that, they can be served up to all age groups. The Mildly Minty Apple Pots are rich in calcium and soluble fiber and taste divine, and as for the rice pudding, once you've made your own, you'll never buy the packaged stuff again!

really rather yummy rice pudding

Makes 4 small portions

⅓ cup brown rice, washed under
    cold water
1¼ cups your baby's usual milk
½ tablespoon sun-dried golden
    raisins
ground cinnamon, to sprinkle

Preheat the oven to 300°F. Lightly grease a small ovenproof dish.

Pour the rice into the prepared ovenproof dish with the raisins and milk. Bake in the preheated oven for 2 hours, or until the rice is cooked. Remove from the oven and let cool slightly. Serve lightly dusted with cinnamon.

Note: For older children, double the quantities, use whole milk or enriched soy milk instead, and flavor with a dollop of high fruit-content raspberry, strawberry, or apricot jam, if desired.

hot apricot semolina

Makes 1–2 portions

4 dried apricots, chopped
1 tablespoon semolina
¾ cup whole milk
1 tablespoon light cream

Wash the apricots and put them in a small saucepan. Cover with boiling water and simmer for 30 minutes, or until very tender, adding more water if necessary. Put the apricots and their cooking water in a blender and whizz until smooth.

Put the semolina and milk in a saucepan. Heat gently, stirring all the time, for about 5 minutes, or until it thickens. Spoon into a bowl, stir in 2 teaspoons of the apricot purée, then finish with a swirl of cream.

mildly minty apple and mascarpone pots

Makes 2 portions

2 apples, peeled, cored, and
    chopped
a sprig of fresh mint
4 oz. mascarpone cheese

Put 2 tablespoons water, the apples, and mint in a saucepan and cook over low heat until the apples have become soft and mushy.

Fold in the mascarpone and serve warm.

12–15 months

quick snacks

Small children sometimes need snacks to keep hunger at bay—they have very small stomachs and are often unable to eat enough calories at mealtimes. However, these snacks must contain fiber, protein, and energy-yielding carbohydrates, not salt, sugars, or saturated fats.

whole-wheat breadsticks with avocado and tomato dip

Makes 10–12, depending on size

1⅓ cups whole-wheat flour
½ cup plus 1 tablespoon white bread flour
½ package (2 teaspoons) fast action dry yeast
2 teaspoons light brown sugar
1 tablespoon extra virgin olive oil
⅔ cup warm water

Avocado and tomato dip
1 small ripe avocado
1 small garlic clove (optional)
1 tablespoon plain yogurt or cream cheese
1 very ripe tomato, diced

2 large baking sheets, lightly greased

Sift the flours in a large mixing bowl (adding the bran left in the strainer) and stir in the yeast and sugar. Make a well in the center and pour in the olive oil, then gradually add the warm water, mixing the flour into the liquid. Mix to form a smooth, pliable dough.

Turn out on a lightly floured surface and mix and knead using your knuckles until the dough feels firm and elastic and is not sticky. Shape into 10–12 balls. Roll on the lightly floured surface into sticks about 3 inches x ½ inch. Arrange on the prepared baking sheets spaced well apart. Cover with lightly oiled plastic wrap and leave in a warm place—out of any drafts—for at least 1 hour, or until doubled in size.

Preheat the oven to 450°F.

Dust the breadsticks with a little white flour and bake in the preheated oven for 12–15 minutes, or until golden brown. Remove from the oven and let cool on a wire rack.

To make the avocado and tomato dip, blend all ingredients in a food processor until smooth, then eat immediately with the warm breadsticks. Store the breadsticks in an airtight container for up to 3 days.

These mini-muffins disappear fast at breakfast, or as snacks with a dollop of Greek yogurt or ice cream. You'll have enough muffins here to eat some fresh from the oven, store a few in an airtight container, and freeze the rest to pull out as and when required. Simply defrost and heat up in a warm oven.

super-healthy blueberry mini-muffins

Makes 20 mini-muffins

1⅓ cups whole-wheat flour
¾ cup white self-rising flour
2 teaspoons baking powder
½ teaspoon baking soda
½ teaspoon ground cinnamon
2 ripe bananas
2 eggs
⅔ cup brown sugar
6 tablespoons polyunsaturated
   margarine
1 teaspoon pure vanilla essence
1 cup ripe blueberries

a mini-muffin pan, lined with
   mini-muffin liners

Preheat the oven to 375°F. Sift together the flours, baking powder, baking soda, and cinnamon in a large bowl.

Peel the bananas and put them in a bowl. Mash them with a fork or purée them with a handheld blender. Add the eggs, sugar, margarine, and vanilla essence and blend again. Pour into the flour mix, and mix until just combined.

Gently fold in the blueberries. Spoon into the mini-muffin liners and bake in the preheated oven for 25 minutes, or until risen and golden brown. Turn out onto a wire rack and let cool. Store in an airtight container for up to 3 days, or freeze.

bango smoothie

Makes 4 portions

1 ripe banana
10 oz. mango flesh, chopped
¾ cup plain yoghurt
¾ cup whole milk
2 teaspoons honey

Peel and chop the banana and put in a blender with the mango, yogurt, milk, and honey. Whizz until smooth. Add more milk if necessary.

Serve immediately.

more super-quick snacks

- Peanut butter spread on whole-wheat pitas, toast, rye bread, or whole-grain crackers (only if your child is not allergic to peanuts, see page 25)
- Chunks of mild cheddar and slices of fresh apple
- Breadsticks and hummus dip
- Cooked pasta pieces
- Whole-grain English muffins spread with mashed banana and cut into quarters

main meals

This ingenious little recipe is packed with vegetables and yet, in my experience, kids simply can't get enough of it! The sauce is so versatile it can be used over pasta mixed with some canned tuna, as a sauce for lasagne, or simply poured over some fried lean ground beef and onions to make a super-quick bolognese.

Makes 4–6 portions

4 oz. lean ground beef
½ small onion, peeled and diced
1 oz. mushrooms, finely chopped
1 garlic clove, crushed
2 tablespoons fresh white bread crumbs
1 teaspoon chopped fresh parsley or thyme
2 teaspoons vegetable oil
1 egg yolk, beaten
1 tablespoon extra virgin olive oil
2 cups couscous
3 cups hot low-sodium chicken or vegetable broth
flour, to coat
sea salt and black pepper

Five-veg sauce
2 tablespoons extra virgin olive oil
1 small onion, peeled and chopped
1 garlic clove, crushed
2 carrots, peeled and chopped
1 small zucchini, chopped
2½ oz. mushrooms, sliced
a 14-oz. can chopped tomatoes
½ cup low-sodium vegetable broth
1 teaspoon dried oregano
½ teaspoon brown sugar

mini-meatballs and couscous with five-veg sauce

Preheat the oven to 350°F.

Put the beef, onion, mushrooms, garlic, bread crumbs, parsley, vegetable oil, egg yolk, and seasoning in a bowl and mix. Shape the mixture into 12 mini-meatballs. Put on a plate, cover, and refrigerate while you make the sauce.

To make the five-veg sauce, heat the olive oil in a saucepan, add the onion and garlic, and sauté for about 3 minutes. Add the carrots, zucchini, and mushrooms and cook for about 15 minutes, or until softened.

Add the tomatoes, vegetable broth, oregano, and brown sugar, season to taste and simmer for 10 minutes. Purée with a handheld blender, then keep over low heat to keep warm.

Put the couscous in a large bowl and pour in the hot broth. Cover and set aside for 5 minutes, or until the couscous has absorbed all the liquid. Fluff up the grains with a fork.

Remove the mini-meatballs from the fridge and lightly dust with flour. Heat the olive oil in a large, heavy skillet and cook the mini-meatballs for 8–10 minutes, turning frequently, until cooked through.

Serve the couscous, mini-meatballs, and sauce together and watch it disappear in no time!

Both of these dishes make really quick, satisfying, and nutritious suppers. And the salad is perfect for lunchboxes or picnics while the Chicken Pieces with Buttery Broccoli Mash is a healthier alternative to the usual sausages and mash. You'll soon discover that most vegetables are great mashed with potatoes.

honey roast ham with golden raisins and cheddar couscous salad

Makes 4–6 portions

1 cup couscous
1¼ cups hot low-sodium vegetable broth
25 seedless grapes, halved
1 cup diced mild cheddar
½ cup golden raisins
½ cup unsweetened apple juice
2 tablespoons chopped fresh flatleaf parsley (optional)
5 oz. honey roast ham, chopped

Put the couscous in a large bowl and pour in the hot broth. Cover and set aside for 5 minutes, or until the couscous has absorbed all the liquid.

Turn the couscous into a cold bowl and fluff up the grains with a fork to separate. Let cool.

Add the grapes, cheddar, golden raisins, apple juice, and parsley and toss together until evenly combined. Serve with the honey roast ham.

pan-fried chicken pieces with buttery broccoli mash

Makes 4 portions

14 oz. potatoes, peeled and cubed
½ low-sodium vegetable bouillon cube, crushed
1 small head of broccoli, florets only
3 tablespoons unsalted butter
2 tablespoons whole milk
1 tablespoon sunflower oil
2 skinless chicken breasts, cubed
sea salt and white pepper

Put the potatoes in a saucepan, cover with water, and add the crushed bouillon cube. Cover with a lid, bring to a boil, then simmer until tender. 5 minutes before the potatoes are ready, remove the lid and put a collapsible steamer on top of the pan. Put the broccoli florets in the steamer, replace the lid, and set aside until both the potatoes and broccoli are soft.

Drain and mash the broccoli and potatoes with the butter, milk, and seasoning. Set aside.

Heat the sunflower oil in a heavy skillet and sauté the chicken pieces for 5–7 minutes, until cooked through and golden brown. Serve with the mash.

Here are two versions of carbonara—one uses smoked trout, which has a high concentration of fatty acids; the other is a simplified carbonara, perfect for when the children are screaming for their dinner and you've just come through the door. You'll be glad to have some, too!

smoked trout and farfalle pasta

Makes 4 portions

6½ oz. farfalle
5 oz. naturally smoked trout fillet (or fresh salmon if unavailable), skinned
1¼ cups frozen peas
⅔ cup light cream
1¼ cups grated Gruyère cheese

Cook the farfalle in lightly salted boiling water according to the manufacturer's instructions. Put a collapsible steamer on the top of the pasta pan and steam the trout for 8–10 minutes.

Remove the trout, flake it with a fork, and set aside. About 3 minutes before the pasta is done, add the peas to the pasta water.

Meanwhile, put the cream and Gruyère in a saucepan and cook over low heat until the cheese has melted.

Drain the pasta and peas and toss with the trout and cheese sauce.

little ones' quick and easy carbonara

Makes 4 portions

8 oz. spaghetti
1 cup frozen peas
2 oz. cooked ham, diced
⅔ cup light cream
⅔ cup grated Parmesan
1 teaspoon unsalted butter

Cook the spaghetti in lightly salted boiling water according to the manufacturer's instructions. About 3 minutes before the pasta is done, add the peas to the pasta water.

Meanwhile, put the ham, cream, Parmesan, and butter in a saucepan and cook over low heat until the cheese has melted. Drain the pasta and peas and stir into the carbonara sauce.

I find that the sweetness of the Ripe Tomato Salsa goes really well with these salmon patties below. Try the salsa with the Cheese Straws on page 63, too. And these sweet potato wedges are so good you'll have to make yourself a few too to stop you stealing them off the kids' plates!

salmon patties, ripe tomato salsa, and sweet potato wedges

Makes 4 portions

1 large sweet potato
4 tablespoons vegetable oil
12 oz. Yukon Gold potatoes
5 oz. salmon fillets, skinned
½ cup grated Gruyère cheese
1 egg yolk
1 tablespoon chopped parsley
½ onion, finely chopped

Ripe tomato salsa
**3 large ripe tomatoes, very
    finely chopped**
½ garlic clove, crushed
2 teaspoons chopped basil
**1 tablespoon extra virgin
    olive oil**

Preheat the oven to 400°F. To make the ripe tomato salsa, mix the tomatoes, garlic, basil, and olive oil in a bowl, cover with plastic wrap, and refrigerate until needed.

Chop the sweet potato into wedges and parboil in a pan of boiling water for 8–10 minutes. Drain and dry off any excess moisture with paper towels. Pour 2 tablespoons of the vegetable oil on a baking sheet and put at the top of the preheated oven for 3–4 minutes, or until the oil is piping hot. Remove from the oven, toss the sweet potato wedges carefully in the oil, and return to the oven for about 30 minutes, or until crisp and crunchy.

Meanwhile, boil half the Yukon Golds in their skins for about 20 minutes, or until cooked but still firm. Drain and let cool.

Cut the salmon into 1-inch chunks and mix with the cheese, egg yolk, parsley, and onion. Peel the cooked potatoes and grate into the salmon mixture. Peel and grate the raw potatoes into a bowl. Shape the salmon mixture into 4 patties then press each one into the raw grated potato until evenly coated. Heat the remaining vegetable oil in a heavy skillet and fry the patties for 3–4 minutes on each side, or until crisp and golden. Serve with the wedges and salsa.

veggie bites

Makes 4 portions

1 small sweet potato, peeled
2½ oz. butternut squash,
   peeled and seeded
5 oz. potatoes, peeled
1 leek, white part only, thinly
   sliced
5 oz. mushrooms, chopped
2 tablespoons chopped fresh
   parsley
1¼ cups fresh bread crumbs
½ tablespoon soy sauce
½ lightly beaten egg
sea salt and black pepper
flour, to coat
1 tablespoon vegetable oil

Grate the sweet potato, squash, and potatoes into a large bowl. Squeeze out some of the excess moisture from the pulp. Add the leek, mushrooms, parsley, bread crumbs, soy sauce, egg, and some seasoning. Mix well.

Form the mixture into about 12 bite-size balls. Sprinkle a little flour on a plate and use to coat each veggie bite.

Heat the vegetable oil in a large, heavy skillet, add the veggie bites, and sauté over medium heat for 8–10 minutes, turning occasionally until golden on the outside and cooked through. Serve. These go well with baked beans.

irish stew with celery root mash

Makes 4–6 portions

4 lamb chops or 1 lb. stewing
   lamb
2 onions, thinly sliced
3 potatoes, peeled and thickly
   sliced
1 tablespoon fresh thyme leaves
5 tablespoons low-sodium
   vegetable broth

Celery root mash
1 tablespoon fresh lemon juice
1 small celery root, peeled and
   cubed
4 potatoes, cubed
a large pat of unsalted butter
black pepper

Trim as much fat as possible from the lamb. Put in a small flameproof casserole dish or a heavy saucepan. Cover with the onions, and top with the potato slices. Add the thyme and vegetable broth. Bring to a boil. Turn the heat right down, cover with a lid, and cook for at least 1½ hours.

In the last 30 minutes of cooking, make the celery root mash. Fill a large saucepan with water and add the lemon juice. Bring to a boil, then add the celery root and potatoes. Bring to a boil again and simmer for 15–20 minutes, or until the vegetables are tender. Drain (reserve the cooking liquid).

Return the potato and celery root to the pan and mash with the butter and a little pepper. Add some of the reserved cooking liquid if necessary to make a creamy purée.

At the end of cooking, the stewed potatoes and onion will have melted into a savory mush and the lamb will be very tender. Pick the meat off the bones (if using lamb chops) and mash it into the vegetables. Make a well in the middle of the mash and fill with Irish stew.

sweets

Mixed Berry Freeze makes a mouthwatering, super-healthy, vitamin-C packed alternative to commercially prepared ice creams, which are usually high in sugars, additives, and saturated fats.

mixed berry freeze

Makes 6–8 portions

9 oz. frozen mixed berries
¼ cup sugar
½ cup grape juice
8 tablespoons heavy cream
2 tablespoons confectioners' sugar

Put the mixed berries in a saucepan with the sugar and grape juice. Simmer for 5 minutes. Purée, then strain and discard the seeds. Let cool.

Stir the cream and confectioners' sugar into the mixed berry purée. Mix well, then transfer to a freezerproof plastic tub and freeze for 1 hour. Beat the mixture with a fork to break up the ice crystals. Freeze again, repeating the beating procedure once or twice during freezing.

rhubarb compote

Makes enough to serve the whole family!

2¼ lb. rhubarb
½ cup sugar
grated peel and juice of 1 unwaxed orange

Preheat the oven to 350°F.

Cut the rhubarb on the diagonal into 1½-inch lengths. Mix with the sugar, orange peel, and juice.

Tip into a large ovenproof dish, cover with aluminum foil, and bake on the middle shelf until just tender, about 25 minutes. Remove the foil and cook for a further 5 minutes. Let cool to room temperature.

Mash roughly with a fork and serve with Greek yogurt. Adults will love it served as a kind of rhubarb "mess" with crushed meringues and cream. Alternatively, spoon some over your porridge for a delicious breakfast. The possibilities are endless!

Both these recipes use white bread. This is partly because it just seems to work better in the recipe and also because too many whole foods and unrefined grains can be very bulky and filling for small stomachs, resulting in a lack of calories and nutrients in a child's diet. White bread is also a good source of calcium.

eggy bread with caramelized bananas

Makes 2 portions

2 whole eggs, plus 1 egg yolk
⅓ cup heavy cream
2 thick slices of white bread,
    crusts removed
a pat of unsalted butter
1 tablespoon sugar
1 ripe banana
Greek yogurt, to serve
honey, to serve
2 tablespoons peanut butter
    (optional)

Preheat the oven to its lowest setting and put a heatproof plate in to warm.

Put the eggs, egg yolk, and cream in a bowl and beat together until combined. Dip the bread slices into the egg mixture to coat.

Heat a nonstick skillet until hot. Dry-fry the eggy bread for 2 minutes on each side or until golden. Place each slice of bread on the warmed plate in the oven.

In a separate skillet, melt the butter and sugar over low heat for about 3 minutes, or until it forms a caramel sauce. Peel and slice the banana diagonally, add to the skillet, and cook until golden brown. Cut the eggy bread into sticks and serve with the caramelized bananas. Drizzle with a little Greek yogurt and honey.

Variation: If your child has no history of peanut allergy, you can spread the bread with smooth peanut butter before dipping into the egg mixture.

yummy plummy bread and butter pudding

Makes 2–4 portions

4–5 thin slices of white bread
1 tablespoon unsalted butter,
    softened
2 ripe plums, pitted and cubed
½ cup brown sugar
3 eggs
2 cups whole milk

*a medium ovenproof dish,
    greased*

Preheat the oven to 350°F.

Spread the bread with a little butter and cut into triangles. Arrange all but 4 triangles in the prepared ovenproof dish along with the plums, then sprinkle with the brown sugar.

Beat the eggs and milk together, then pour most of it into the dish. Place the remaining triangles of bread on top and brush with the remaining egg mixture. Let stand for 30 minutes, then put in a roasting pan half-filled with hot water.

Put in the preheated oven and cook for 45–50 minutes, or until the egg mixture is set.

Note: This can be frozen after cooking. Reheat in the oven until thoroughly hot.

double quick, double chocolate dessert

Makes 2 portions

2 small, ripe bananas
8 oz. silken tofu
2 teaspoons cocoa powder
**a square of bittersweet
    chocolate**

Silken tofu is available at most supermarkets. It is soft and creamy in texture and can be used for dips, spreads, sauces, and sweet dishes. As well as having a high protein content it also contains calcium and iron, and is rich in B vitamins. To maximize the antioxidants in this dessert, use the best-quality cocoa powder and chocolate with at least 70 per cent cocoa content.

Peel the bananas, roughly chop, and pop in a food processor with the tofu and cocoa powder. Whizz until you get a smooth purée.

Put into serving bowls. Carefully shave the chocolate using a cheese grater and sprinkle over the desserts.

These are two tasty little desserts to satisfy a sweet tooth without overloading your child with sugar. Adults with a child's taste for sweet things will love them too.

oatmeal pots with warm strawberry sauce

Makes 4 portions

4 tablespoons fine or medium
   ground oats
¾ cup whole milk
½ sweet apple, peeled and cored
4 tablespoons heavy cream
4 strawberries, hulled and
   sliced, to decorate

Strawberry sauce
8 oz. strawberries
1 tablespoon fresh lemon juice
2 tablespoons sugar, or to taste

Put the oats and milk in a small bowl and grate in the apple. Stir, cover, and refrigerate for about 8 hours.

To make the strawberry sauce, put the strawberries, ⅔ cup water, the lemon juice, and enough sugar to taste in a heavy saucepan. Heat gently, stirring occasionally, until the sugar has dissolved. Bring to a boil, reduce the heat, and simmer for 5 minutes, or until the strawberries are really soft.

Purée the stewed strawberries in a blender, then strain to get a smooth sauce.

Put 1 heaping tablespoon apple and oat mixture into a small bowl with a tablespoon of cream and pour over the warm strawberry sauce. Decorate with the sliced strawberries.

raspberry egg custards

Makes 4–6 portions

1⅓ cups heavy cream
¾ cup whole milk
6 egg yolks
3 tablespoons honey
3½ oz. ripe raspberries,
   plus extra to serve
freshly grated nutmeg
sugar, to serve

4–6 small heatproof bowls
* or ramekins*

Preheat the oven to 325°F.

Put the cream and milk in a heavy saucepan and heat until almost boiling, then remove from the heat and let cool slightly.

Beat the egg yolks and honey together in a heatproof mixing bowl, then pour in the hot cream.

Divide the raspberries between the small bowls and pour over the egg custard mixture. Sprinkle with freshly grated nutmeg. Put the bowls in a roasting pan half-filled with hot water. Put in the preheated oven and bake for 50–60 minutes, or until just set.

Remove the bowls from the oven and let cool. Refrigerate until half an hour before serving. Serve topped with ripe, fresh raspberries and a sprinkling of sugar.

Apples, pears, and blackberries are all in abundance in the fall months, which makes these desserts ideal comfort foods for your little ones to settle down to as the evenings draw in. These fruits are all great sources of fiber, too, helping to ensure a healthy digestive system.

apple and blackberry crumble

Makes 6–8 portions

2 large cooking apples, peeled, cored, and chopped
6½ oz. blackberries
fresh juice of 1 lemon
½–⅔ cup sugar
1½ cups all-purpose flour
1 teaspoon baking powder
3 tablespoons ground almonds
5 tablespoons unsalted butter, cubed
3 tablespoons rolled oats
custard (see below), vanilla ice cream, or yogurt, to serve

a medium pie dish, greased

Preheat the oven to 350°F.

Mix the apples, blackberries, lemon juice, and 3–4 tablespoons sugar to taste in the prepared pie dish.

Mix the flour, baking powder, and ground almonds together in a large bowl. Add the butter and rub in with your fingertips until the mixture resembles fine bread crumbs. Stir in ⅓ cup of the sugar and the oats.

Spread the crumble over the fruit and bake in the preheated oven for about 30 minutes, or until the top is golden brown. Serve with custard, vanilla ice cream, or yogurt.

custard and pear pudding

Makes 6–8 portions

6½ oz. canned pear halves, cubed
5 tablespoons unsalted butter, softened
6 tablespoons sugar
1 egg
½ cup plus 1 tablespoon all-purpose flour
a drizzle of honey

Custard
2 large egg yolks
1 tablespoon pure maple syrup
1 heaping teaspoon cornstarch
1 teaspoon pure vanilla essence
1¼ cups whole milk or enriched soy milk

Preheat the oven to 375°F.

Divide the chopped pears between 6–8 small bowls or ramekins. Cream the butter and sugar until pale. Add the egg, beat well, then fold in the flour.

Divide the mixture between the ramekins, place the ramekins onto a large baking sheet, and bake in the preheated oven for 20–30 minutes.

Meanwhile, to make the custard, beat the egg yolks, maple syrup, cornstarch, and vanilla essence in a heatproof bowl. Put the milk in a saucepan and heat gently until warm. Pour into the egg mixture. Stir, return to the pan, and keep stirring over low heat until the mixture coats the back of a spoon or reaches your desired consistency.

Remove the pear puddings from the oven and let cool for a few minutes, then serve warm with the custard.

toddlers

quick snacks

Fill hungry bellies with these easy, zingy little lemon cakes. Lemon is a strong flavor for a young palate, but these treats are a great way of introducing children to a new taste that they might otherwise reject, and the yogurt and cream cheese make them rich in calcium, too. They are ideal for packed lunches or with a glass of ice-cold milk for older children.

Makes 15–20 cakes

3 tablespoons plain yogurt
½ cup sugar
3 tablespoons unsalted butter, melted
1 egg
finely grated peel of ½ unwaxed lemon
1 cup self-rising flour

Frosting
3½ oz. cream cheese
1 tablespoon confectioners' sugar
1 tablespoon fresh lemon juice

a mini-muffin pan, lined with mini-muffin liners

mini yogurt and lemon cakes

Preheat the oven to 350°F.

Whisk together the yogurt, sugar, butter, egg, and lemon peel, then fold in the flour. Spoon the mixture into the mini-muffin liners and bake in the preheated oven for 30 minutes, or until a skewer inserted into the center of the cakes comes out clean. Let cool slightly, then transfer to a wire rack to finish cooling.

Meanwhile, to make the frosting, cream the cream cheese, confectioners' sugar, and lemon juice together until smooth then use to top each cake.

Cheesy Sardine Subs are almost like mini-pizzas so they'll go down well, plus the sardines contain omega-3 fatty acids needed for healthy brain development and a strong immune system. Active toddlers will benefit from the Avocado Dip with Roast Chicken Dippers, full of heart-protecting monounsaturated fats and protein.

cheesy sardine subs

Makes 4 subs

2 soft sub rolls
1 small can of sardines in tomato sauce
1 teaspoon dried mixed herbs
1 tablespoon tomato paste
1 teaspoon red wine vinegar
grated mild cheddar or soy cheese, to taste

Preheat the broiler to medium-hot.

Slice the sub rolls in half horizontally and toast lightly under the preheated broiler.

Put the sardines, herbs, tomato paste, and vinegar in a small bowl and mash.

Spread the mixture onto the subs, sprinkle lightly with cheese, and pop back under the broiler until the cheese is melted and golden brown. Serve with a glass of ice-cold milk.

avocado dip with roast chicken dippers

Makes 6 portions

1½ tablespoons extra virgin olive oil
3 small chicken breasts, skinned
2 ripe avocados
fresh juice of 1 lime
1 garlic clove, crushed
1 tablespoon finely grated Parmesan
1 plum tomato, seeded and finely chopped
1 tablespoon diced red onion
2 tablespoons diced cucumber
sea salt and black pepper

Preheat the oven to 400°F.

Heat ½ tablespoon of the olive oil in a skillet until very hot and sear the chicken breasts. Put the chicken on a baking sheet, season to taste, then roast in the preheated oven for 12–15 minutes, or until cooked through and the juices run clear. Remove from the oven and let cool slightly.

Meanwhile, halve the avocados, discard the pits, and scoop the flesh into a food processor with the lime juice, garlic, and remaining olive oil. Process until smooth and transfer the purée into a bowl.

Fold in the Parmesan, tomato, onion, and cucumber, and season with pepper. Cut the chicken into strips and serve with the dip.

creamy tomato and bacon soup

Serves 4–6

2 tablespoons extra virgin
   olive oil
1 onion, diced
1 garlic clove, crushed
1 large carrot, peeled and grated
3 lean smoked bacon slices,
   finely chopped
a 14-oz. can of chopped
   tomatoes
¾ cup low-sodium chicken broth
2 teaspoons red wine vinegar
1 bay leaf
a sprig of fresh thyme
6 tablespoons heavy cream
sea salt and black pepper

Heat the olive oil in a large saucepan. Sauté the onion, garlic, carrot, and bacon for 5 minutes.

Stir in the tomatoes, broth, vinegar, bay leaf, and thyme. Cover and simmer for 35–40 minutes.

Remove the bay leaf and the stalk from the thyme, returning the thyme leaves to the pan. Blend in a food processor until smooth.

Stir in the cream, and season to taste. Serve with chunks of warm whole-grain bread or buttered oatcakes (see page 63).

Note: This soup can also double up as a sauce over pasta, couscous, or mixed beans.

Toddlers' tummies are small so it's not always feasible for your little ones to get all the calories they need in just three main meals per day. These healthy bakes will help boost your child's calorie and nutrient intake without all the saturated fats, refined sugars, and additives that often come with commercially prepared alternatives.

date and seed bars

Makes 10–12 bars

1 cup chopped dried dates
1¼ cups old-fashioned rolled oats
3 tablespoons sunflower seeds (ground in a food processor)
1 cup whole-wheat flour
½ cup light brown sugar
1 teaspoon baking powder
⅓ cup hazelnuts, very finely chopped
8 tablespoons unsalted butter, softened

an 11 x 9-inch baking pan, greased

Preheat the oven to 350°F.

Put the dates and ¾ cup water in a saucepan and bring to a boil. Reduce the heat and simmer gently for 20–25 minutes, or until the dates are tender and most of the liquid has been absorbed. Blend in a food processor or blender until smooth. Set aside.

Put the oats, sunflower seeds, flour, sugar, baking powder, and hazelnuts in a bowl and mix well. Add the butter and mix in with your fingertips until well combined.

Put three-quarters of the mixture into the prepared baking pan and press down to make a smooth, even layer. Spread the date mixture evenly over the top. Sprinkle over the remaining oat mixture and press down lightly. Bake in the preheated oven for 20–25 minutes.

Let cool in the pan, then cut into bars and serve. Store in an airtight container for 3–4 days.

whole-wheat yogurt and raisin scones

Makes 12 large or 24 mini-scones

1⅔ cups whole-wheat flour
1 teaspoon salt
1 teaspoon baking soda
2 tablespoons margarine
5 oz. plain yogurt
¼ cup brown sugar
⅓ cup raisins
a little milk, to glaze

a 2-inch plain cookie cutter

Preheat the oven to 425°F.

Put the flour, salt, and baking soda in a bowl. Rub in the margarine, then stir in the yogurt, sugar, and raisins to make a soft dough. Roll out on a lightly floured surface to ½ inch thick and cut into rounds with the cookie cutter.

Put the rounds on a baking sheet and brush with a little milk. Bake in the preheated oven for 7–10 minutes until well risen and golden brown.

Remove from the oven, let cool slightly, then cut in half and spread with margarine and a little high fruit-content jam.

main meals

If your children like sausages and meatballs they'll love this. It's a real favorite in my family and the children love to get involved with making the beef patties too. If possible, make twice the quantity of patties, individually wrap the extras you don't use, and freeze them to use on those busier days.

pan-fried mini beef patties with sautéed collard greens

Makes 12 mini beef patties

2 tablespoons vegetable oil
1 small onion, peeled and diced
4 oz. lean ground beef
½ teaspoon dried thyme
6½ oz. potatoes, peeled and
    boiled for 12 minutes,
    then mashed together with
    2 tablespoons unsalted butter
1 tablespoon chopped fresh
    parsley
1 tablespoon tomato ketchup
a dash of Worcestershire sauce
a little flour, to dust
a pat of unsalted butter
6 large collard green leaves,
    shredded
reduced-salt, reduced-sugar
    baked beans, to serve
    (optional)
sea salt and black pepper

Heat 1 tablespoon of the vegetable oil in a saucepan and fry the onion for 3–4 minutes. Add the beef and fry for a further 3–4 minutes. Stir in the thyme and season to taste. Cook for another minute.

Stir the mixture into the mashed potato with the parsley, tomato ketchup, and Worcestershire sauce. Let cool, then cover and refrigerate until cold.

Form the mixture into 12 little patties, dust with flour, cover, and refrigerate for another hour.

Heat the remaining vegetable oil in a large skillet and sauté the patties for about 5 minutes, or until golden and cooked through.

Melt the butter in a large, heavy skillet, add the shredded collard greens, and sauté for 4–5 minutes, stirring frequently.

Serve the patties and collard greens with baked beans on the side (if using).

Chunky Tuna Frittata is just as tasty made with haddock, mackerel, or salmon, or even lean ham. This and the soup (in a mini-thermos) work well in older children's lunchboxes instead of the usual sandwiches.

Makes 4–6 portions

2 tablespoons extra virgin olive oil
1 small onion, thinly sliced
1 garlic clove, finely chopped
2 tablespoons diced red bell pepper
6½ oz. tuna canned in sunflower oil, drained and flaked
3 cups peas
5 large eggs, lightly beaten
2 tablespoons heavy cream
2 tablespoons grated cheddar

chunky tuna frittata

Preheat the broiler to medium-hot.

Heat the olive oil in a heavy, ovenproof skillet over medium heat. Add the onion, garlic, and bell pepper, stir-fry for 3–4 minutes, then stir in the tuna and peas.

Mix the eggs and cream and pour into the pan mixture. Cook until the base of the frittata is set (about 5–7 minutes).

Remove from the heat, sprinkle with the cheddar, and place under the preheated broiler. Cook the top of the frittata for 3–4 minutes, or until set and lightly golden. Remove from the broiler and let rest for 5–6 minutes. Serve the frittata warm with cherry tomatoes on the side.

sausage and bean hotpot

Heat the olive oil in a large saucepan, add the sausages, and cook over low heat for 10 minutes, or until evenly brown, then remove from the pan and set aside.

Add the bacon and onion to the pan and cook for 5 minutes, then add the garlic and cook for a further minute.

Add the tomato purée, cannellini beans, paprika, and sugar, then season and mix well. Return the sausages to the pan, bring to a simmer, and cook everything together for a further 15 minutes. Check that the sausages are thoroughly cooked—if not, simmer for a little longer until they are ready.

pea and bacon soup

Heat the olive oil in a saucepan. Add the onion and cook over medium heat for 5–6 minutes, or until softened but not colored. Add the garlic and cook for a further minute.

Stir in three-quarters of the peas, then pour in the broth. Bring to a boil and simmer for 10–12 minutes. Meanwhile, preheat the broiler to medium-hot.

Broil the bacon until crisp.

Let the soup cool for a few minutes, then transfer to a food processor and whizz until smooth. Return the soup to the pan and add the remaining peas. Bring to a boil and simmer for 2 minutes.

Break the bacon into bite-size pieces and scatter over the soup. Serve with chunks of bread.

Children seem to love pancakes so these savory pancakes are a treat, especially as the buckwheat flour is gluten-free and rich in amino acids and B vitamins. Ham, pea, and parsley work very well but these pancakes can be filled with tomato-based sauces, tuna, smoked salmon and cream cheese, chicken, or shredded duck.

ham, pea, and parsley pancakes

Makes 6 pancakes

1 tablespoon butter, melted
1 cup whole milk
½ cup buckwheat flour
½ cup all-purpose flour, sifted
a pinch of salt
2 eggs
vegetable or olive oil, for frying

Sauce
2 tablespoons unsalted butter
2 tablespoons whole-wheat flour
1¼ cups whole milk
1 tablespoon very finely chopped parsley
1 cup peas, cooked
6½ oz. roast ham, finely chopped

a crêpe pan or nonstick skillet

Preheat the oven to its lowest setting and pop in an ovenproof plate to warm up.

Stir the butter into the milk. Put the flours and salt together in a mixing bowl, or into a food processor bowl. Beating all the time, pour in the milk and butter mixture, then add the eggs one at a time until everything is blended well. Let rest in the fridge for at least 30 minutes.

Brush the crêpe pan with a little oil and set it over medium heat. When the oil is smoking, pour a ladleful of batter into the pan and tilt it around until it is evenly spread. When the underside is golden, turn the pancake over and cook the other side for 1–2 minutes.

Slide the pancake out of the pan onto paper towels on the warmed plate and keep warm in the oven while you make the rest of the pancakes. Re-oil the pan between each pancake.

To make the sauce, melt the butter in a small saucepan, remove from the heat, and stir in the flour. Return the pan to the heat and cook, stirring for 1 minute. Gradually add the milk, stirring constantly until the sauce has thickened. Add the parsley, peas, and ham and cook for a further 3–4 minutes.

Serve each pancake filled with a tablespoon or two of the sauce.

Super-quick, Cheatin' Mini-pizzas are the answer to nutritious fast food when faced with children so hungry they simply can't wait for the real thing. The Smoked Mackerel and Zucchini Mornay is a great variation on fish pie. It freezes well too, so make up extra quantities if you can, to use on the days you don't have time to cook.

super-quick, cheatin' mini pizzas

Makes 4 portions

4 whole-grain English muffins
⅔ cup tomato purée
toppings of your choice, such
as diced ham, pineapple, corn
kernels, flaked tuna, sliced
mushrooms, bell peppers, and
shredded fresh herbs, etc.
½ cup grated mozzarella or mild
cheddar

Preheat the oven to 400°F.

Slice the muffins in half horizontally. Spread the tomato purée over them, then top with any toppings of your choice, or simply with a little grated cheese.

Bake in the preheated oven for 8–10 minutes until the muffins are crispy round the edges and the cheese is golden and bubbling.

smoked mackerel and zucchini mornay

Makes 4 portions

14 oz. potatoes, peeled and
cubed
1 large carrot, diced
6½ oz. mackerel canned in
sunflower oil, drained and
flaked
6½ oz. smoked mackerel fillet,
skinned, boned, and cubed
2 hard-boiled eggs, halved
1 large zucchini, sliced
1 tablespoon polyunsaturated
margarine
2 tablespoons heavy cream
½ cup grated mild cheddar
2 ripe tomatoes, sliced

Sauce
2 tablespoons unsalted butter
2 tablespoons whole-wheat
flour
1¼ cups whole milk
½ cup grated mild cheddar

Preheat the oven to 350°F.

Put the potatoes in a saucepan, cover with water, and boil for approximately 20 minutes, or until soft. Meanwhile, steam the carrots for 3–5 minutes.

Put the canned mackerel, smoked mackerel, eggs, carrots, and zucchini in an ovenproof casserole dish and mix well. Set aside.

Remove the potatoes from the heat, drain, add the margarine and cream, and mash until completely smooth.

To make the sauce, melt the butter in a small saucepan, remove from the heat, and stir in the flour. Return the pan to the heat and cook, stirring for 1 minute. Gradually add the milk and cheddar, stirring constantly until the sauce has thickened and the cheddar has melted.

Pour the sauce into the casserole and top with the mashed potato. Sprinkle with the cheddar and arrange the tomatoes on top. Bake in the preheated oven for 20 minutes, or until golden.

herby trout packages

Makes 4 portions

8 sheets of phyllo pastry
a little extra virgin olive oil,
to brush
4 skinless and boneless
trout fillets
1 scallion, finely chopped
1 teaspoon chopped cilantro

This dish is a great way of getting kids to eat oily fish. Besides, it's good from time to time to expand their horizons and offer them something a little different from what they usually eat. You can use salmon instead of trout if you like.

Preheat the oven to 375°F.

Brush two sheets of phyllo pastry on both sides with olive oil and place them carefully one on top of the other. Repeat with the remaining sheets.

Put a trout fillet on top of a pair of phyllo sheets, and sprinkle over a quarter of the scallion and cilantro. Roughly roll up the trout, then fold the phyllo pastry over the trout to make a triangular package. Put seam-side down on a baking sheet and bake in the preheated oven for 20–25 minutes until cooked through.

Remove the packages from the oven and let cool slightly before serving with boiled new potatoes and sugar snap peas.

warm cherry tomato and basil tartlets

Makes 4 portions

**10 oz. ready-made puff pastry,
  thawed if frozen**
¾ cup tomato purée
1 cup cherry tomatoes, halved
4 teaspoons ready-made pesto
**a little extra virgin olive oil,
  to drizzle**
a handful of fresh basil leaves

Preheat the oven to 400°F.

Roll out the puff pastry on a lightly floured surface to about ¼ inch thick. Cut out six rounds about 5 inches in diameter using a small plate or bowl as a guide.

Place on a lightly floured baking sheet and gently press down the edges with your finger, then prick all over with a fork. Bake in the preheated oven for 5 minutes then remove from oven.

Spread each round with the tomato purée, lay the cherry halves on top, cut-side down, then dab the tartlets with 1 teaspoon pesto each. Drizzle with a little olive oil then return to the oven and bake for a further 10 minutes until the pastry is golden.

Serve warm sprinkled with basil leaves. The tartlets go well with cottage cheese.

Bell peppers are rich in the antioxidant vitamins A, C, and E and red peppers additionally contain lycopene, a natural pigment that is particularly valuable in protecting against cancer—which makes these Roast Polenta-stuffed Bell Peppers a wholesome feast.

roast polenta-stuffed bell peppers

Makes 4 portions

**3 cups low-sodium chicken or
    vegetable broth or water**
**2 cups polenta or stone-ground
    cornmeal**
**6 mixed bell peppers (red,
    yellow, and green), halved
    and seeded**
8 oz. mozzarella, thinly sliced
**finely grated cheddar,
    to sprinkle**
sea salt and black pepper

Preheat the oven to 350°F.

Put the broth in a large saucepan and bring to a boil. Gradually pour in the polenta, stirring constantly. Cook over low heat for 25–30 minutes, until the polenta is almost too thick to stir.

Place the bell pepper halves hollow-side up on an oiled baking sheet and fill each one with the polenta. Bake in the preheated oven for 45 minutes. Remove from the oven and place the mozzarella slices on top of each pepper, then sprinkle with the cheddar. Bake for a further 5 minutes, or until the cheese begins to melt.

Arrange 3 different colored peppers on each serving plate and serve with fish, chicken, or roast ham.

mozzarella-topped herby vegetable loaf

Makes 6–8 portions

8 oz. carrots, grated
1 red onion, finely chopped
2 garlic cloves, crushed
3 celery ribs, finely chopped
4 oz. mushrooms, sliced
1 small zucchini, sliced
1 tablespoon chopped parsley
2 tablespoons chopped cilantro
⅔ cup grated mild cheddar
2 eggs
1 cup whole-wheat flour
1½ cups grated mozzarella

Sauce
3 tablespoons extra virgin
   olive oil
½ onion, sliced
1 garlic clove, crushed
1 teaspoon sugar
two 14-oz cans chopped
   tomatoes
sea salt and black pepper

a 1-lb loaf pan

This recipe is a bit like a veggy version of meatballs in tomato sauce. Eat it as it is or serve it with a little pasta or new potatoes and peas or broccoli on the side.

Preheat the oven to 350°F. Line the loaf pan with parchment paper.

Mix all the loaf ingredients except the mozzarella in a large bowl. Spoon into the prepared loaf pan and bake in the preheated oven for 1 hour.

Meanwhile, to make the sauce, heat the olive oil in a saucepan. Add the onion and garlic, cover with a lid, and cook over gentle heat until soft and pale golden.

Add the canned tomatoes (with all the juice) to the onion mixture. Stir in the sugar and season to taste.

Cook, uncovered, for about 30 minutes, or until the tomato softens.

Remove the loaf from the oven and let stand for 5 minutes. Preheat the broiler to hot.

Tip the loaf out onto a plate and slice. Put the slices into a shallow, ovenproof dish. Pour over the tomato sauce and sprinkle with grated mozzarella. Broil for 4–5 minutes, or until the cheese is bubbling and golden. Serve immediately.

sweets

Gooseberries are a good source of fiber and vitamins A and C. This Gooseberry Fool uses white grape juice concentrate for sweetness and the rich creaminess of Greek yogurt to take away the berries' characteristic tart and tangy taste.

gooseberry fool

Makes 6–8 portions

2 pints green or pink gooseberries, topped and tailed
⅓ cup frozen white grape juice concentrate or apple juice concentrate, thawed
1¼ cups Greek yogurt

Put the gooseberries in a saucepan with ¼ cup water and bring to a boil. Simmer over low heat for 15 minutes, or until the gooseberries have softened.

Mash the gooseberry mixture with a fork. Stir in the white grape juice concentrate and let cool. Layer Greek yogurt and gooseberry purée in glasses or bowls and refrigerate until needed.

wholesome honey and apple cake

Makes 8 portions

7 tablespoons polyunsaturated margarine
¾ cup dark brown sugar
3 eggs, beaten
1¾ cups whole-wheat flour
1 teaspoon apple pie spice
2 teaspoons ground cinnamon
2 teaspoons baking powder
1 lb. cooking apples, peeled, cored, and finely chopped
2 tablespoons honey
4–6 tablespoons whole milk

a deep 9-inch cake pan, lined with greased parchment paper

Preheat the oven to 325°F.

Cream together the margarine and sugar until light and fluffy. Add the eggs, a little at a time, beating constantly.

Sift together the flour, apple pie spice, cinnamon, and baking powder. Add to the egg mixture along with whatever's left in the strainer, mixing thoroughly. Fold in the apples, 1 tablespoon of the honey, and enough milk to produce a soft dropping consistency. Pour into the prepared cake pan and bake for 1½ hours, or until well risen and firm to the touch. Meanwhile, warm the honey slightly in a saucepan.

Turn the cake out onto a wire rack and let cool slightly. Pour the warmed honey over the cake. Serve as a snack with a glass of ice-cold milk or as a dessert with custard (see page 99).

Kids will enjoy making these easy hotcakes as much as eating them so get them involved. Don't be afraid to try out different toppings like strawberries and cream or blueberries mixed with Greek yogurt and honey. The crumble is more wholesome than its traditional recipe with the added oats and ginger.

buttermilk hotcakes
with bananas and maple syrup

Makes 15–20 hotcakes

2 cups all-purpose flour
1 teaspoon baking soda
2 teaspoons cream of tartar
1 tablespoon sugar
2 eggs
1 teaspoon sunflower oil
1¼ cups buttermilk
unsalted butter, for frying
slices of banana, to serve
a drizzle of pure maple syrup,
  to serve

Put the flour, baking soda, cream of tartar, and sugar in a bowl and make a well in the center. Add the eggs, oil, and half of the buttermilk to the well and gradually incorporate the flour with a whisk. Add the remaining buttermilk and beat well to make a smooth batter.

Melt a big pat of butter in a large, heavy skillet. Drop large spoonfuls of batter into the skillet from the tip of the spoon to form rounds, spacing well apart. Cook for 2–3 minutes until bubbles appear on the surface and burst, then turn them over and cook for a further 1–2 minutes until golden brown underneath. Put the hotcakes on a clean kitchen towel and fold it over to keep them warm while you cook the rest of the hotcakes.

Serve the hotcakes warm, topped with slices of banana and a generous drizzle of maple syrup.

pear, ginger, and coconut crumble

Makes 4–6 portions

5 ripe Comice pears, peeled,
  cored, and chopped
1 inch fresh ginger, finely grated
½ cup whole-wheat flour
½ cup dried coconut
½ cup rolled oats
8 tablespoons polyunsaturated
  margarine, cubed
6 tablespoons brown sugar

Preheat the oven to 350°F.

Put the pears and ginger in the bottom of a casserole dish and stir thoroughly.

Put the flour, coconut, oats, margarine, and sugar in a bowl and mix with your fingertips until it resembles bread crumbs. Sprinkle on top of the pears and bake for 30–40 minutes until the top begins to brown. Remove from the oven and let cool slightly, then serve warm with a dollop of good-quality ice cream.

peach and almond tarts

Makes 8–10 tartlets

¾ cup plus 2 tablespoons
    whole-wheat flour
⅓ cup ground almonds
a pinch of salt
2½ tablespoons sugar
6 tablespoons polyunsaturated
    margarine
1 egg, beaten
plain yogurt, to serve
cubes of fresh peach, to serve
pure maple syrup or honey,
    to serve

a tartlet tray, well greased

Almonds have the highest protein content of any nut as well as being rich in the minerals magnesium, potassium, and phosphorous, and especially high in calcium. They are also high in monounsaturated fat so really, these tartlets are positively good for you!

Preheat the oven to 375°F.

Mix the flour, almonds, salt, and sugar together in a bowl and rub in the margarine. Mix in the egg to form a soft dough.

Roll out the pastry thinly on a lightly floured surface. Cut into 8–10 circles to fit your tartlet tray. Arrange in the tray and bake in the preheated oven for 15 minutes. Let cool.

Fill each tartlet with a dollop of yogurt, then top with the peaches and drizzle with maple syrup.

Store any remaining tartlet cases in an airtight container for up to 2 days, or freeze in batches of 4–6 and warm up in the oven. Try other fillings, such as sliced strawberries mixed with a little elderflower cordial and served with a spoonful of whipped cream.

family meals

beef bourguignon

Serves 4 (adults)

Sautéed Collard Greens for the adults (see page 108)
1 tablespoon extra virgin olive oil
1½ lb. beef chuck or bottom round steak, cubed
2 onions, peeled and chopped
2 carrots, peeled and chopped
1 garlic clove, crushed
a 14-oz. can chopped tomatoes
1¼ cups low-sodium vegetable broth
2 teaspoons chopped fresh herbs of your choice
1 tablespoon tomato paste
5 oz. button mushrooms
sea salt and black pepper

The beef and the collard greens make this an iron-packed dish, one that tastes so good I have often served it at mid-winter dinner parties. However, although it may sound very sophisticated and grown up, just a few little alterations make it an ideal dish for the younger members of the family, too.

Preheat the oven to 375°F.

Heat the oil in a flameproof casserole dish. Add the beef cubes and cook until evenly brown. Remove from the casserole and set aside.

Add the onions, carrots, and garlic to the casserole and cook until softened.

Return the beef to the casserole along with the tomatoes, broth, herbs, tomato paste, and some seasoning. Bring to a boil. Cover with a lid and cook in the preheated oven for 1½ hours.

Add the mushrooms and return to the oven, still covered, for a further 30 minutes.

For your baby: Purée or chop with some plain steamed cabbage and some mashed potatoes.

For your toddler: Spoon a little onto a plate with some plain steamed cabbage and some mashed potatoes.

For the adults: Add a glass of red wine to the casserole at the end of cooking and simmer for a further 20 minutes. When you sauté the cabbage, add 2 slices of bacon, finely chopped. Stir 1 teaspoon horseradish sauce per person into the mashed potato.

chili con carne

Serves 4 (adults)

8 oz. ground beef
2 tablespoons extra virgin
   olive oil
1 onion, finely chopped
1 carrot, finely chopped
1 red bell pepper, seeded and
   finely chopped
1 garlic clove, crushed
1 tablespoon mixed dried herbs
a 14-oz. can chopped tomatoes
⅔ cup low-sodium beef broth
sea salt and black pepper

This is another dish that is effective in boosting iron levels (the mineral most likely to be lacking in adults and children) because the vitamin C in the tomatoes helps to enhance the body's ability to absorb the iron from the beef.

Heat a heavy skillet and add half the ground beef. Dry-fry over high heat to color the meat, breaking up any lumps with the back of a fork. Repeat with the rest of the beef and drain off any fat.

Heat the olive oil in a separate saucepan and cook the onion, carrot, and red pepper until they start to soften.

Stir in the garlic and the herbs and cook for 2 minutes. Stir in the tomatoes and the broth and season well. Add the beef and simmer gently for 40–50 minutes until thick.

For your baby: Purée and serve with plain white or brown rice.

For your toddler: Spoon a little onto a plate, stir in a little cream if desired, and serve with a tablespoon of plain white or brown rice.

For the adults: Add a small can of kidney beans, 2 tablespoons chili powder, and a glass of red wine at the end of cooking. Simmer for a further 15–20 minutes. Serve with brown rice or nachos, 1 tablespoon guacamole, and 1 tablespoon sour cream per person.

really easy chicken risotto

Most children like rice and chicken so this dish is usually pretty popular with the kids. However, add a little smoked pancetta and Parmesan and serve the risotto with a fresh arugula, cherry tomato, and balsamic salad and a glass of cold Sauvignon, and you'll have a winner with the adults too!

Serves 4 (adults)

2 tablespoons extra virgin
   olive oil
1 red onion, finely chopped
2 garlic cloves, finely chopped
1½ cups risotto rice
4 skinned and boned chicken
   thigh fillets, halved
2 teaspoons chopped fresh
   rosemary
4¼ cups hot low-sodium
   chicken broth
a pinch of saffron strands
sea salt and black pepper

Preheat the oven to 425°F.

Heat the olive oil in a flameproof casserole dish and sauté the red onion and garlic until soft. Stir in the rice, chicken, rosemary, broth, saffron, and some seasoning, and cook in the preheated oven for 30 minutes, or until the rice is tender and the chicken cooked through.

For your baby: Purée a little of the risotto and some of the chicken in a food processor, adding a splash of your baby's usual milk or a little extra vegetable broth if required.

For your toddler: Shred the chicken with your fingers, mix into 1–2 tablespoons of the risotto, and stir in a drizzle of light cream.

For the adults: Pan-fry 1–2 tablespoons finely diced pancetta, stir into the risotto, and top with 1 tablespoon grated Parmesan per person.

foil-baked salmon and couscous

You really don't get an easier meal to make than this. Once you've put all the ingredients in the foil bag (which not only seals in all the flavors, making everything taste truly delicious, but also removes the need to add any extra fat in the cooking process) and popped it in the oven, there's nothing to do until 20 minutes later when it's ready to eat.

Serves 2 adults, 1 toddler, and 1 baby

2 cups couscous
2 zucchini, thinly sliced
2 carrots, finely chopped
1½ tablespoons frozen peas
1½ tablespoons corn kernels
1 lemon
2 cups full-flavored vegetable broth
3 salmon fillets

Preheat the oven to 350°F.

Mix the couscous, zucchini, carrots, peas, and corn together in a bowl.

Fold a large sheet of aluminum foil or parchment paper in half and tightly fold one open side to seal. Holding the open "bag" in one hand, carefully tip in the couscous mixture. Cut the lemon in half and squeeze the juice from one half into the broth. Cut the remaining half into slices.

Lay the salmon on top of the couscous and top with the lemon slices. Tightly fold over another open side of the bag, then carefully pour in the broth.

Fold the remaining open side tightly. Bake in the preheated oven for 20–25 minutes, depending on how thick your fish is, until the fish is cooked and the couscous is fluffy.

For your baby: Purée some salmon, couscous, and vegetables together with a little of your baby's usual milk or vegetable broth.

For your toddler: Flake some salmon into the couscous mixture and serve warm.

For the adults: Add a teaspoon of lemon peel to the cooked couscous, mix well, then serve on warm plates topped with a salmon fillet per person.

flaked haddock moussaka

Serves 4 (adults)

12 oz. undyed haddock fillets, skinned and diced
1 teaspoon fresh lemon juice
4 zucchini, thinly sliced
2 eggs
1¼ cups light cream
a pinch of freshly grated nutmeg
a little fresh dill, finely chopped
½ cup grated mild cheddar
⅓ cup finely grated Parmesan (optional)

a shallow ovenproof dish, greased

This is one of those meals that is extremely comforting in the winter served with some sautéed collard greens, and yet works equally well in the summer alongside a large green salad.

Preheat the oven to 375°F.

Check the haddock very carefully for any remaining bones and discard them. Put the fish in the prepared baking dish and sprinkle with the lemon juice.

Steam the zucchini in a collapsible steamer over a pan of boiling water. Remove from the steamer, pat dry, and layer over the fish.

Beat the egg and cream together, stir in the nutmeg, dill, and cheddar and pour over the fish and zucchini. Sprinkle with the Parmesan, if using. Put the dish in a small roasting pan half-filled with cold water. Bake in the preheated oven for about 45 minutes, or until the top is golden.

For your baby: Put a small portion of the moussaka in a food processor and purée to the desired consistency.

For your toddler: Serve with Sweet Potato Wedges (see page 88).

For the adults: Serve with mashed potatoes mixed with fresh chives.

websites and sources

American Academy of Family Physicians
www.familydoctor.org
Everything you might need to know about your family's health, including a section on kids and nutrition.

American Academy of Pediatrics
www.aap.org
141 Northwest Blvd
El Grove Village, IL 60007
847-434-4000
Authoritative website dedicated to the health of all children.

Center for Science in the Public Interest
www.cspinet.org
Suite 300
1875 Connecticut Avenue NW,
Washington DC 20009
202-332-9110
Offers information on nutrition.

Children's Hospital Boston
www.childrenshospital.org/az/Site1753/mainpageS1753P0.html
Tips and suggestions for feeding your toddler.

Dr. Spock
www.drspock.com
A section on infant feeding provides plenty of advice about what feeding equipment you need, controlling mealtime behavior, food safety, snacking etc.

Earth's Best
www.earthsbest.com/baby_nutrition/home.php
Lots of useful articles about toddler nutrition.

KidsHealth.org
Website for parents and kids covering everything from birth to nutrition; reviewed by doctors and sponsored by the Nemours Foundation Center for Children's Health.

Keep Kids Healthy
www.keepkidshealthy.com
A comprehensive guide to children's nutrition answering all your questions about feeding.

Mayoclinic.com
www.mayoclinic.com
Features advice on babies' and children's health.

The New Parents Guide
www.thenewparentsguide.com
Online resource for parenting information. Includes baby feeding equipment such as highchairs, bottles, bibs, etc.

Zero to Three
www.zerotothree.org
National Center for Infants, Toddlers, and Families
2000 M St., NW, Suite 200
Washington, DC 20036
800-899-4301 (toll-free)
202-638-1144
Nonprofit organization that promotes healthy development of babies and children. Also offers an online A–Z of parenting.

index

conversion charts

**Weights and measures have been rounded up or down
slightly to make measuring easier.**

1 stick butter   8 tablespoons   125 g

Volume equivalents

American	Metric	Imperial
1 teaspoon	5 ml	
1 tablespoon	15 ml	
¼ cup	60 ml	2 fl oz
⅓ cup	75 ml	2½ fl oz
½ cup	125 ml	4 fl oz
⅔ cup	150 ml	5 fl oz (¼ pint)
¾ cup	175 ml	6 fl oz
1 cup	250 ml	8 fl oz

Weight equivalents

Imperial	Metric
1 oz	25 g
2 oz	50 g
3 oz	75 g
4 oz	125 g
5 oz	150 g
6 oz	175 g
7 oz	200 g
8 oz (½ lb)	250 g
9 oz	275 g
10 oz	300 g
11 oz	325 g
12 oz	375 g
13 oz	400 g
14 oz	425 g
15 oz	475 g
16 oz (1 lb)	500 g
2 lb	1 kg

Measurements

Inches	Cm
¼ inch	5 mm
½ inch	1 cm
¾ inch	1.5 cm
1 inch	2.5 cm
2 inches	5 cm
3 inches	7 cm
4 inches	10 cm
5 inches	12 cm
6 inches	15 cm
7 inches	18 cm
8 inches	20 cm
9 inches	23 cm
10 inches	25 cm
11 inches	28 cm
12 inches	30 cm

Oven temperatures

225°F	110°C	Gas ¼
250°F	120°C	Gas ½
275°F	140°C	Gas 1
300°F	150°C	Gas 2
325°F	160°C	Gas 3
350°F	180°C	Gas 4
375°F	190°C	Gas 5
400°F	200°C	Gas 6
425°F	220°C	Gas 7
450°F	230°C	Gas 8
475°F	240°C	Gas 9

acknowledgments

The publisher would like to say thank you to all the lovely
children who modeled for this book: Annalise, Bea, Charlie,
Drew, Elena, Emelia, Faheem, Giovanni, Jonathan, Polly & Ruby.

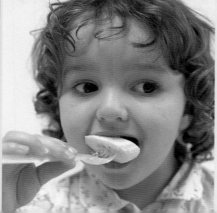